MY FINAL TERRITORY

For Zenya,
best
wishes —

[signature]

11 | 15 | 18

My Final Territory

Selected Essays

YURI ANDRUKHOVYCH

*Translated by Mark Andryczyk
and Michael M. Naydan,
with one essay translated
by Vitaly Chernetsky
Edited and with annotations
by Michael M. Naydan*

UNIVERSITY OF TORONTO PRESS
Toronto Buffalo London

© University of Toronto Press 2018
Toronto Buffalo London
www.utppublishing.com
Printed in the U.S.A.

ISBN 978-1-4875-0171-6 (cloth)

♾ Printed on acid-free, 100% post-consumer recycled paper with vegetable-based inks.

Library and Archives Canada Cataloguing in Publication

Andrukhovych, Yuri, 1960–
[Essays. Selections. English]
My final territory : selected essays / Yuri Andrukhovych ; translated by Mark Andryczyk and Michael M. Naydan, with one essay translated by Vitaly Chernetsky ; edited and with annotations by Michael M. Naydan.

Includes bibliographical references and index.
ISBN 978-1-4875-0171-6 (hardcover)

1. Andrukhovych, Yuri, 1960– – Translations into English. I. Andryczyk, Mark, 1969–, translator II. Naydan, Michael M., 1952–, editor III. Chernetsky, Vitaly, translator IV. Title.

PG3949.1.N37A2 2018   891.7'944   C2017-905131-8

  Канадська
фундація
українських
студій

Canadian Foundation
for Ukrainian Studies
Fondation canadienne
des études ukrainiennes

This publication was made possible in part by the financial support of the Canadian Foundation for Ukrainian Research

University of Toronto Press acknowledges the financial assistance to its publishing program of the Canada Council for the Arts and the Ontario Arts Council, an agency of the Government of Ontario.

 Canada Council
for the Arts
Conseil des Arts
du Canada

ONTARIO ARTS COUNCIL
CONSEIL DES ARTS DE L'ONTARIO
an Ontario government agency
un organisme du gouvernement de l'Ontario

Funded by the   Financé par le
Government   gouvernement
of Canada   du Canada

 Canada

Contents

Acknowledgments

Part of "The Central-Eastern Revision" appeared previously under the title "Within Time, Down a River" in the journal *AGNI*; "Carpathologia Cosmophilica" appeared first in *Trafika Europe*; and "Love and Hatred in Kiev" was published in *The New York Times* international edition.

A Biographical Preface about the Author[1]

Yuri Andrukhovych is one of today's pre-eminent Ukrainian writers and intellectuals and the leading representative of postmodernism in Ukraine. He was born in 1960 in the Western Ukrainian city of Ivano-Frankivsk (formerly called Stanislaviv) near the foothills of the Carpathian Mountains. The older name of his native city gave rise to what Volodymyr Yeshkilev and subsequent literary critics have called The Stanislav Phenomenon, which includes a coterie of outstanding writers and artists from Stanislaviv-Frankivsk. Andrukhovych's early education included intensive study of German, which would serve him well later in close ties to Germany. He received his undergraduate degree in journalism in 1982 from the Polygraphics Institute in Lviv, a multicultural city that became a central locus of his literary activity. After completing his undergraduate degree he was conscripted into the Soviet army from 1983 to 1984, worked for various newspapers, and in the final years of the existence of the USSR received a stipend for postgraduate studies in 1989–91 at the prestigious Maxim Gorky Literary Institute in Moscow. He earned a Candidate's Degree (PhD equivalent) in Ukrainian philology in 1996 at the Precarpathian University in Ivano-Frankivsk, writing his dissertation on the great Lemko-Ukrainian poet Bohdan Ihor Antonych, whose life and aesthetic attitude to his poetic craft have deeply inspired Andrukhovych.

Andrukhovych began his literary career as a poet and has published six books of poetry – *The Sky and City Squares* (1985), *The Downtown* (1989), *Exotic Birds and Plants* (1991), *Exotic Birds and Plants with an Addendum "India"* (1997), *Songs for a Dead Rooster* (2004), and *Letters to Ukraine* (2013). Andrukhovych's poetry (after his first two more

traditional books of poetry) like that of the Beat Poets whom he translated, is largely bombastic, taboo-breaking, and iconoclastic. Many
of his poems have been turned into extremely popular rock songs by
now-classic Ukrainian rock bands Plach Yeremii (Jeremiah's Cry) and
Mertvyi Piven (Dead Rooster).

Andrukhovych is the anointed "Patriarch" of the extraordinarily
influential Bu-Ba-Bu literary performance group that he founded in
1985 together with the poet Viktor Neborak and the satirist Oleksander
Irvanets. The name of the group is formed from the first two letters of the
Ukrainian words meaning buffoonery (*bufonada*), farce or puppet show
(*balahan*), and burlesque (*burlesk*). Strongly influenced by Mikhail Bakh-
tin's notion of carnival, Andrukhovych and his Bu-Ba-Bu co-members
strove to create not just staid readings of their writings but performances of their works that became more and more lavish over time
and drew larger and larger crowds in the late1980s and early 1990s,
culminating in the grand Chrysler Imperial "happening" at the Lviv
Opera House in 1992. All three members of Bu-Ba-Bu infused their live
readings with showmanship: art works and multimedia visuals; rock,
rap, and jazz music; and other performative elements, all with a high
degree of parody and an attitude of carnivalization.

Andrukhovych's first prose works were published in 1989 and
included vividly realistic short stories based on army life. Andriy Don-
chyk's film *Oxygen Starvation* (1991) was based on his stories. The author
shifted his creative output primarily to longer-form prose writing in 1992
when he published his first novel *Recreations*, the plot of which follows
the then popular Ukrainian penchant for organizing large Woodstock-
like outdoor music and cultural revivals like the Chervona Ruta festival, which is named after an immensely popular song by Volodymyr
Ivasiuk, a popular Ukrainian composer who had been murdered by
the KGB in 1979. The novel was just as bombastic as Andrukhovych's
poetry, with its candidly raw depiction of youth culture rife with sex and
alcohol use, topics that were banned in the USSR in pre-independence
Ukraine. The novel was attacked by ultraconservative critics and
praised by more open-minded ones. Like much of Andrukhovych's
writing, it immediately garnered a near cult following by the younger
readership in Ukraine. Andrukhovych released his second novel,
The Moscoviad, in 1993, which is based largely on the author's experiences in Moscow during his postgraduate studies. The novel deals
with the end times of the crumbling Soviet empire, in which Moscow
seems like a hellish place doomed to destruction. Candid depictions

of sexuality and some of the more raw aspects of youth culture also infused the novel.

Andrukhovych's third novel, *Perverzion* (1996), comprises his tour de force as a writer. It received the novel of the year award for 1996 from the pre-eminent Kyiv-based journal *Suchasnist*, which recognized his talent as a writer early on and introduced many of his works to a Ukrainian audience. The plot of *Perverzion* consists of an attempt to solve the disappearance of Lviv performance poet Stanislav "Stakh" Perfetsky, a close friend. It consists of a miscellany of variegated narratives, of different versions and *per*versions: first-person, third-person, surreptitiously heard and seen narration, recorded narration (video- and audiotapes), diaries, computer files, and published artefacts. In many respects the novel is voyeuristic because the reader has access to the most intimate details of the poet's life. I have noted elsewhere that the novel can be regarded as somewhat of a postmodernist saint's life in genre, with technological innovations providing the means for gathering information, giving the reader both filtered and unfiltered access to moments in Perfetsky's life and allowing the reader to determine which versions ring truest. The novel also can be read as a philosophical novel, in many ways like Bulgakov's *The Master and Margarita*, to which it has been compared. *Perverzion* deals with the powerful questions of life and death, of killing or not killing, of the immortality of the soul, of good versus evil, of Hamletian being or not being. It is also an intimate and profound love story, with Ada (aka Cerina in her role as the secret agent monitoring Perfetsky's activities) central to the plot. Rather than giving answers to the unanswerable questions, the novel, in postmodernist fashion, gives choices, possibilities, and impossibilities. Before writing the novel Andrukhovych had visited Venice for just one day, but was so enthralled by the visit that he voraciously acquired extensive knowledge of the city through guidebooks and other resources. With its linguistic innovativeness, multifaceted styles, and playfulness, the novel truly represents the epitome of literary carnival in its Ukrainian postmodernist manifestation.

Andrukhovych's novel *The Twelve Circles* (2003) shifted away from the intensely parodic style of *Perverzion* and returned to more traditional modes of narration. The novel follows the fate of Austrian photographer Carl-Josef Zumbrunnen from his native Vienna to his travels through Western Ukraine where he finds love, various adventures, death, and even the afterlife. The novel was criticized by some for fancifully drawing parallels between the hero and Lemko-Ukrainian poet Bohdan Ihor Antonych, and by others for being so different and sober compared with Andrukhovych's initial trilogy of carnivalized Bu-Ba-Bu works.

Andrukhovych's most recent novel (if one can call it that) is his highly autobiographical *A Mystery: Instead of a Novel* (2007). Its plot revolves around seven days of interviews recorded with Andrukhovych by German journalist Egon Alt (critics have noted the similarity to the Latin expression *alter ego*), who dies before publishing them. The author collects these tapes, and transcribes and publishes them, relating various moments and aspects of his own life. His later book *Lexicon of Intimate Cities* (2011) is in the genre of New Journalism and comprises memoiristic writing about 111 cities the author visited during his creative lifespan.

Over virtually his entire literary career Andrukhovych has been actively engaged in journalistic activities and essay-writing. In the 1990s, together with Yuri Izdryk, he edited and published the innovative journal *Thursday* (Chetver) and honed his essay-writing skills as a columnist for the Kyiv newspaper *The Day*, writing a column under the rubric Park of Culture. Andrukhovych also edited the Internet literary almanac *Train #76* (its name derives from a train that travels from Ukraine to Poland) for several years in the first decade of the twenty-first century. An engaging essayist, whose focus is on Ukrainian space and identity within the wider context of Europe and the world, Andrukhovych published a number of his contemplative culturological essays in a volume in 1999 under the title *Disorientation in Location*. He later collected and published his essays and columns under the titles *My Europe* (2000; with Polish writer Andrzej Stasiuk), *The Devil Is Hiding in the Cheese* (2006), and most recently *Fantomas is Buried Here* (2015). One feature unifies all of Andrukhovych's writings in every genre – hybridity. Even in his essays readers can find a polyphony of styles and literary devices.

An extremely active cross-cultural facilitator, Andrukhovych has translated, among other works and authors, Shakespeare's *Hamlet* and *Romeo and Juliet*, and the poetry of the New York School of poets and the Beats, the latter under the title *The Day Lady Day Died* (2006). He has also translated Rainer Maria Rilke and Robert Walser from German, Tadeusz Konwicki and Bruno Schulz from Polish, and Boris Pasternak and Osip Mandelstam from Russian.

Since 2005, Andrukhovych has been vigorously involved with live performance and recording with the experimental Polish musical group Karbido. In addition to touring live with the group on numerous occasions, he has released three CDs based on his poetry with them in both Polish and Ukrainian editions: *Moonshine* (2006, 2008), *Cinnamon, with the Addendum of India* (2009, 2010), and *Atlas Estremo* (2015); and a CD/DVD project, *Absinthe* (2012), advertised as a "media spectacle" when performed live on tour, based on his novel *Perverzion*.

Andrukhovych's works have also been presented on stage in Germany, Poland, and in Ukraine. In 2007, a Youth Theatre Ukrainian-German joint production of the play *Orpheus the Illegal*, based on scenes from the novel *Perverzion*, had its debut in Dusseldorf, Germany, with Andrukhovych himself playing a role in the play. The Youth Theatre staged a play after that based on *The Moscoviad*. Andrukhovych's *Hamlet* premiered at the Golden Lion International Theatre Festival in Lviv in 2010. And in 2011 the Polish Theatre of Dance staged a play based on Andrukhovych's novel *The Twelve Circles*.

Andrukhovych has received numerous prizes for his writing, including: the prestigious Herder Prize in Literature in 2001, the Antonovych Prize in Literature that same year, the Erich Maria Remarque Peace Prize (2005), the Leipzig Book Fair Prize (2006) for European mutual understanding, the Angelus Prize for his novel *Twelve Circles* (2006), the Hannah Arendt Prize (2014), and a Goethe Medal (2016) for his promotion of German culture in Ukraine. His works have been translated into a number of languages, including Bulgarian, Czech, English, Finnish, French, German, Polish, Russian, and Swedish.

Andrukhovych continues to live in Ivano-Frankivsk on the physical periphery (of Ukrainian political life and culture) which gives him the aesthetic distance he needs as an artist. His constant travels take him as a cultural ambassador throughout Ukraine, Europe (especially Poland and Germany), and North America, yet he has always remained an engaged citizen who has actively participated in the Orange (2004) and Euromaidan (2014) Revolutions in his homeland. Andrukhovych's earlier controversial pronouncements, for which he was vehemently attacked, calling for Ukraine to abandon the Donbas before the armed conflict there began, now seem prescient. His invited speeches to the European Parliament during the Euromaidan crisis and his continued stance in his writings all call for freedom, democracy, and an end to corruption in Ukraine, ethical postures that Andrukhovych, citizen of the world, has always promoted.

A Note on Yuri Andrukhovych's Most Personal Essay

I remember not being particularly enamoured of Yuri's title for the original, much shorter version of the lengthy essay included here ("Central Eastern Revision"), which was published under the title "Within
Time, Down a River" in the literary journal *AGNI*. Yet over time I have
learned to appreciate that original title more and more. It deals with
two concepts: the first abstract and conceptual (time) and the second
concrete but metaphorical (a river). Two directions are inherent in that
title, too, "Within" being centripetal and "Down" suggesting movement forward. The new title of this much expanded version of the essay
"Central Eastern Revision" focuses less on the metaphorical and more
on concrete location, the latter of which still informs the former, yet also
orients us in locality (to play with the title of one of Yuri's other essays,
"Disorientation in Location").

To the point of becoming somewhat of a cliché, time, since the dawn
of ancient philosophical thought, has invariably been compared to a
river, one that inexorably moves forward but never back. And rivers
in ancient beliefs often must also be crossed to transcend the corporeal
world into that of the spirit. Yet there is one caveat to the time-as-a-
river metaphor. Memory and contemplation do allow thoughtful think-
ers like Andrukhovych to navigate that river of time in both directions
and to probe the past for illumination and self-definition. For what
else is a life other than all the points and experiences remembered in
time between birth and death, between beginning and end, relived in
our minds, and sometimes, as in this case, written down for others to
read, to contemplate, and to understand for themselves? Everything
in between those two linear beginning and endpoints comprises what
makes us who we are as human beings.

For Andrukhovych's essay, and for virtually all his published works,
locality is paramount, be it Moscow – the hellish capital of the crumbling Soviet empire in *The Moscoviad* (1993); Venice, the birthplace of
carnival, in the novel *Perverzion* (1993); the city of Lviv and Galician
Western Ukraine in the novel *The Twelve Circles* (2004); or his more recent
book of 111 essays, *Lexicon of Intimate Cities* (2011), on cities and local-
ities he has visited around the world. A sense of being is profoundly
linked to one's origins in time and space, to one's peregrinations, and
these essays are all about time, place, and peregrinations.

The essay, just like Andrukhovych's fanciful novel *Perverzion*, deals
with philosophical questions that have tormented humanity since the

dawn of time. These include: the nature of time itself, life and death, mortality and immortality, consciousness, memory, self- and national identity, and the ambivalent nature of the violence of war, displacement, and family. Regarding the latter, this essay, first and foremost, comprises a family chronicle of the Andrukhovych family from its darkest days of existential crisis during times of war when life was held to a thread by chance, and then follows the heritage passed down both in large and small ways from grandfather to father to son. In Andrukhovych's chronicle, the relics of the past, the ruins of buildings, civilization, and nature, the aging and infirmity of the body, the ruins brought about by time, all have stories to tell. And the artful storyteller and thinker tells them here.

Some of the most poignant moments in the essay consist of Andrukhovych's depiction of his father's death and funeral. That narrative moves from the inner numbness of psychological shock upon learning of his father's death, to the mechanical making of funeral arrangements with indifferent people for whom death is commonplace and just their daily bread, to a stream of consciousness automatic form of writing that just conveys scraps of what the eyes see and the ears hear in that state.

Another aspect of Andrukhovych's writing that particularly strikes me is the fact that as an intellect he is so well-read and informed about both the historical and wider contemporary world, whereas that wider world knows little about him and his homeland, Ukraine. The essays in this volume give the Anglophone reader the opportunity to see what makes Andrukhovych tick as a human being outside of the masks of his characters and narrator. However, the reality of his nonfiction can also illuminate aspects of the fictions created by one of the most dynamic writers from the new expanded Europe of today.

– Michael M. Naydan, Woskob Family Professor of Ukrainian
Studies, The Pennsylvania State University

En Route Endeavours

Most of Yuri Andrukhovych's essays translated for this volume are culled from two of his publications – *Dezorientatsiia na mistsevosti* (Disorientation in Location [1999]) and *Diavol khovaiet'sia v syri* (The Devil Is Hiding in the Cheese [2006]).[1] These books are subtitled *sproby* (attempts), emphasizing the origins of the genre – the French *essayer*. In fact, these essays, or attempts, strongly suggest that they comprise part of an ongoing work that will continue to appear in various forms in the future.

All of these essays consist of approaches from different angles at defining Ukraine's place on the Map of the World, mostly inspired, in fact, by the many travels undertaken by the author since the collapse of the Soviet Union in 1991. In taking on geography, Andrukhovych largely focuses on his native region, Halychyna (Galicia) in Western Ukraine, as he tries to fit it onto several different maps. With maps you have borders and with borders you have neighbours and Andrukhovych's intellectual excursions sketch the contours of Ukraine's relationships with its neighbours (and between them), first and foremost Poland and Russia. His essays dash through ruins and stumble over traces of empires – most important, the Austro-Hungarian Empire of which Galicia was a part – and demonstrate how they have influenced Ukrainian language, culture, and identity. Andrukhovych's innovation lies in his ability to approach significant topics through a highly engaging and witty narrative that offers his particular carefully layered blend of the historical, the whimsical, and the personal.

Andrukhovych's frequent journeys have also led to much contact with the West. Some of these essays are the texts of actual speeches the writer was asked to deliver at gatherings of intellectuals, both in Ukraine and abroad. At meetings beyond the borders of Ukraine, Andrukhovych has represented the living embodiment of the existence of the Ukrainian language. His essays provide an insider's view of such meetings at which Western intellectuals met to discuss this suddenly accessible, strange, and knotty realm of Eastern and Central Europe, offering depictions of Westerners in Ukraine and Ukrainians in the West.

Taken together, these essays are, in essence, travels through language, along language, and about language. They are an essential component of the writings of one of Ukraine's leading authors. And like Yuri Andrukhovych's poems and novels, his essays are now available in English translation, journeying on trajectories to ever more corners of the World.

– Mark Andryczyk, Columbia University

Author's Introduction

Upon giving English-language readers for their perusal this collection of texts, which were written in the freest of literary genres, I first and foremost give sincere thanks for this opportunity to my translators and publishers. For me personally, the essay is my favourite genre. I had literary debuts with it in German, Polish, French, and Spanish linguistic spaces. The fact that a collection of my *attempts* has not yet appeared in English has, I must say, caused me a certain amount of disappointment. So it is good that from this point forward, this dark age, so to speak, is now behind me.

As I approached my very first essay, "Introduction to Geography" (1993), which is not included in this collection, I was already quite well known in Ukrainian reading circles as a poet and novelist. The former role was associated primarily with the poetic Bu-Ba-Bu trio, which has now been a legend for a long time. Michael Naydan writes about it quite extensively in his introduction, so I will not go into detail here. I note only that it was the most beautiful adventure of my youth. And the most fateful, too.

The latter role as writer arose from the fact that I had just published my first two novels: *Recreations* (1992) and *The Moscoviad* (1993). Both publications were accompanied by scandals of moderate intensity that could not help but contribute to underscore the popular opinion of me as a hell-raiser and provocateur. Many readers received my first essay precisely from this point of view. Frankly, I had no objections to that.

The opportunity to take on the essay genre came as a result of my first and relatively long (three month!) stay in the West. It was a stipend from the city of Munich to writers from Eastern Europe to go to a quite paradisal place in the foothills of the Bavarian Alps. I am offering so much detail on the circumstances of time and place because their impact on my succeeding formation as a writer turned out to be downright stunning. And all that I wrote over subsequent years and decades can be considered a direct result of those three months in early 1992.

It probably happened because I was subconsciously preparing myself for Europe (or more widely – for the West) as for a universal and polyphonic cultural complex and – again subconsciously – set out as my aim with all my strength to drag into it my culturally tormented and in a literal sense impoverished country, which at that time mostly did not know (and sometimes did not want to know) its place or path.

All my *attempts*, which you will find in this book, are primarily about seeking a place and path. That is why we, together with My Translators, decided to select for it a series of my earlier essays written before the now distant year 2000. And that is why they are presented here primarily in chronological order, according to their time of writing.[1] Perhaps this will allow you to at least somehow reconstruct my geopoetical expeditions in their most logical sequence.

So, treat this book not as a collection of individual essays, but as an autobiographical novel that was written over the course of a quarter century.

With gratitude for your attention.

Yuri Andrukhovych
29 July 2016
(Translated by Michael M. Naydan)

MY FINAL TERRITORY

Autobiographical Essay

The Central-Eastern Revision[1]

TRANSLATED BY MICHAEL M. NAYDAN

1
A Roadside Death Notice[2]

Since my childhood I've been drawn to ruins, I could repeat after Danilo Kiš.[3]

From my childhood I've been drawn to ruins, that special trace, that special garden of previous being. I don't want to explain this away as some kind of metaphysical or romantic inclinations. Maybe the reason for this has been just the scent, and not any particular kind of Geist. Decaying dampness, something purely physiological. Old walls, rotting beams, half-decayed things have only their own kind of breath – could it be, maybe, I'm a toxicoholic?

Thank God, the landscape of my part of the world is sufficiently permeated with these kinds of objects. Old ruined houses, entire blocks in the maws of the downtowns of cities, neglected, tattered, nooks of courtyards suffused with mould and urine, stairwell cages of buildings covered with autumn leaves – it turns out some lushes still happen to live there, entire communes of lushes with the true inner spirit of communism. It happens, too, that they're driven out from there, the legalized bourgeoisie is buying up real estate as quickly as possible, conquering territories, class warfare continues, the elementary accumulation of capital the same, an anachronistic life according to Marx takes on new postmodern variations, but ruins remain ruins.

I grew up in the world of these kinds of small town courtyards and houses, of these verandas and garrets that were in fashion a hundred years ago. Yes, literally a hundred years ago, for I'm speaking about the previous fin de siècle, about the turning point of two eras, which in the provinces generally had not been perceived as demonically, say, as in Vienna. The larger part of this world today lies in ruins, but I still remember those strange, slightly stooped old men and women who cursed in their Galician dialectisms, who knew their high school Latin sayings and in the times of Khrushchev and the Beatles dressed as though they had come out to greet the Archduke Franz Ferdinand. How did they manage to preserve that clothing – that's the question! In spite of all the purges, house searches, deportations, nationalization?

I remember their old scent – nothing out of the ordinary, just the scent of an old body, it's just different. Weariness, illnesses, and troubles collect in a person over the years, and afterward that special scent appears, a symptom of collapse.

Difference distinguished them in everything – by the time of my childhood they already seemed to have been extraterrestrials, they were tormented by sclerosis, migraines, and manias, a badly mastered Russian. Or did a complete disorientation in everyday social relations give them away in all this standing on their ears?

It seemed as if they had become some kind of secret society, some kind of esoteric Bruno Schulz Kaiser-König Club, although all their secretiveness was much too obvious and completely non-functional, as though it were the use of their already mentioned Latin proverbs. In childhood I loved to spy on them, for their bird-like facial expressions. Or to mimic their language, all those distortions of sound, intonational dislocations, lexical curiosities. I very much disliked them, evidently sensing an inner prevalence of death within their organisms, and that repelled me. Later they appeared in my nightmares – with bags and walking sticks, along with their scent of oldness.

But I've gotten too carried away with these shadows. For my love of ruins is not limited to old downtown zones.

2
Concrete Poetry

One rainy summer many years ago my friends and I were hiking along some vine-covered foothills, trying to find old ruined castles. We were college students and craved everything in the world: impressions, friendship, sex, wine, music. Since we didn't have that much money with us, we just gave all this – the wine, the music – to each other. We could only guess that a decade earlier young people in the West must have tried something like this and that, apparently, it had brought them just more disillusion and clinical maladies. But what was the West for us then? From time to time it sent us sound signals in the form of contraband music. In everything else it didn't, in fact, exist, this was a fabrication of our ideologues, some kind of Antiworld, a Contrary World from the evening telecast, *the dark side of the Moon*.

So we were left to hike along the castles on this side of the border. We searched for at least a fragment, at least a hint of something distant, of some Italy-France-Germany, but no – it was not this that we sought, but rather news about the fullness of being. About the fact that it consists of a visible and invisible part – and that second one is the primary and decisive one. A little later I read Rilke, who wrote about "the bees of the invisible," who gather "invisible honey," so, we assume, that during that rainy summer we were those gatherers of honey.

It seemed to us that the very ruins of the castles contain within themselves "something distant," news about that fullness. The castle ruins were fragments of some long past "complete" world. Among them there was even a Templar one, a castle of the knights of the Temple, the easternmost in Europe of the rose garden of the troubadours. From the surrounding villagers we bought cheap home-made wine (they had only red and white for some reason), then we drank it up somewhere among the ruins, overgrown with burdocks and lilies, the scent of ever-present castle excrement blended in with a thousand other summer scents (for a complete enumeration of the plants see the floral handbooks that are at least a hundred years old, but not later ones). The wine also tasted best when we mixed the red with the white. Rain also passed us as quickly as it began. We ordered on-demand manifestations of shows for ourselves – the flight of sparrows, the appearance of wet dogs, or, for example, a rainbow, and right then and there we got it, everything including the rainbow. We followed it from the embrasures and windows, from the ramparts, from the gates and from the moats – for it's at the age of twenty when people manage to do such temporary tricks.

Yes, absolutely, this was something very temporary and very fleeting, between a comic and a book of naive wisdom, these hikes of ours, these overnight stops, these rickety buses, these foothill villages with foreign dialects (we were really the foreigners and were immediately exposed).

And the wine of ruins.

Yes, of course, the comics prevailed. Or some kind of totally adolescent TV series, first kisses. But I lived through this, I was there. And it was good for me there. So much so that even right now I want to remain there, to be stuck on this page, to be caught in the frames of this second chapter – and not go anywhere, not write anything else, to halt the river. I can remain there, I yearn to be frozen there on the spot, in the old embrasure beneath the sparrows and rainbows. (Someone somehow informed us all about the "death of the author," so here is its variant: textual euthanasia.)

But what then would happen with all the rest of my after-twenty future (past?) life, with all my poems, my books, my actions? With all these springs, hopes, flops, and sheer drops. Where can it find itself, this life?

3
Glossary

The previous question, surely, is worthy of being left without an answer.

Instead I'll return to the topic of ruins. This will be something in the form of a register or a slightly expanded catalogue of all other ruins of this world. "All" – here, clearly, I've exaggerated my possibilities, but let it be so: those at least that I remember.

First of all for some reason industrial ruins come to mind: abandoned factories, all types of junk and scrap iron, railroad tracks, some kind of smokestacks, train cars standing still, mine shafts and tunnels covered over, radiation, rust, halted mechanisms, brick smashed to smithereens, burnt shells of buildings, absurd assembled "installations." All this landscape catastrophe is the flip side of the idiocy of industrial production.

Of course the ruins of ancient civilizations are – cities in jungles, temples inhabited now by monkeys, wells now populated by reptiles.

Farther there are the ruins of roads. Once in the mountains I was walking along just such a road; it was stone and grass, grass and stone, but I knew that five or six decades ago this was a road, and men and women moved along it in coaches and cabriolets. The entire time children babbled hysterically, and maidservants barely managed to catch up to them on foot with baskets in their hands brimming with food.

In addition, obviously, there are ruins of bridges, those once strong pilings that for some reason are called "bulls" in my country, maybe for their stubbornness: impertinent engineering masterpieces that remained amid the course of the river water.

The aqueducts, perhaps, also belong here, that is, their ruins.

You also come across ruins of rivers themselves – water that no longer flows. In the somewhat phantasmagoric city of Lemberg-Lvov-Lviv there is a river that became the city's sewer. In the sixteenth century sailboats from the Baltic Sea, from Danzig and Lübeck passed through it, and you could nearly catch the snakelike Sargasso Atlantic eels with your bare hands. Today it exists just in the sewer pipes, beneath the cobblestones and asphalt. In fact I've heard that eels can survive even in sewer pipes. There's also life beneath the asphalt, the German maximalists of 1968 used to say.

There are also ruins of seas, mostly deserts, but what are they to us? Ruins of forests, lakes, mountains, and stones.

Then there are ruins of ships – those that lie on the bottom (the "Titanic," ladies and gentlemen, certainly, but not just the "Titanic" – entire flotillas, fleets!), but also those that are tossed out onto the shore, among them one found by Buendia Marquez amid the Amazon rain forest, at a distance of a four-day walk from the seacoast, a Spanish galleon; perhaps, too, remains from rocket ships belong here, as do chunks of meteorites.

There are also ruins of cemeteries, especially there where genocide took place, purges, and mass deportations. Because one certainly can settle in other people's residences and take their wardrobes, dishware, linen, or gold teeth for yourself, but no one will go to look after someone else's dead. Much less tend after someone else's graves. I've seen precisely these kind of ruins – Jewish, Armenian, Lemko. To read the names from the slabs with your hands you have to tear off the moss. I have a fair idea where the ghetto used to be in my town. Andrzej Stasiuk once showed me a strange street – a stony forest road; the forest was to the right and left, forest and only forest everywhere, but this was the main street of a Lemko village with the telling name of Charne (Black).

Besides this, there must be ruins of languages, words, ruins of letters, of this movable memory.

Here, however, I prefer to pause. By mentioning languages and words, it's as though I'm crossing a certain boundary, and from a real topical concreteness I'm leaping to a world of shaky abstractions; and this may be totally undesired, for in this way one can begin to speak about the ruins of souls, conscience, feelings, honesty-decency-fidelity, chastity, virtues, the ruins of love and the ruins of hate, the ruins of faith, the ruins of expectations.

Thus I would be forced into moralizing (in fact, I've already begun), into breaking into open doors and windows, into creating some kind of anxious draft in these corridors between the past and the future.

Instead of this I would prefer to look more circumspectly at objects and things, at everything that is palpable. My childhood dream of becoming an archaeologist sometimes returns. I write poetic accounts about dumpsters and ruined houses, about the cellars and garrets cluttered with medieval, pardon me, middle-European rubbish. Considerably more telling than any moral maxims appear to me to be simply the shards of an old mode of life: artificial flowers, vases, Christmas tree angels with lambs, worn-out coins, any kind of decadent jewellery, frayed garters, music boxes, birds' nests. Old aquariums interest me, petrified fish, soot-covered bathtubs and basins, of course, bottles excite me, all kinds of bottles in various erotic forms and bents, male and female bottles in various colours, of various sizes, especially those in which the scent of wine drunk aeons ago or liqueurs has not been aired out! I have a special love for geographical maps that intimate the Edge of the Earth, turtles and whales, about the Sea on the spot of the present-day Carpathians, about dormant Carpathian volcanoes, and also about all kinds of forgotten local formations, for example, Bohemia, Galicia, or Cisleithania.[4] After them I should also mention century-old railroad timetables – of course I've been late for every one of them, but it's important for me to know that there were two trains from Lemberg to Venice and the first of them went through Vienna-Innsbruck, and the second through Budapest-Belgrade.

I also am taken with piles of ancient papers, rolls of legal complaints and documents, sempiternal periodicals, the yellow of newspapers and books, which are turned from right to left, street signs with inscriptions in one of the imperial languages, portraits of Emperor Franz Josef, any kind of portraits and engravings, phonograph records, off of which neither Caruso nor any recent tenor with the Italian name of Pavarotti will no longer sing, theatrical or circus tickets for performances completely and long disappeared into oblivion, postcards from colonies, trendy resorts or the front lines, cards for playing canasta, bridge or poker, tarot cards, picture postcards with facsimile autographs of silent film idols or famous serial killers.

My allergy reacts to this painfully: dust and disintegration, disintegration and dust. And all the same, again and again I plunge into these thickets – as though there is still something there besides disorder.

Yes, all this is disintegration and dust. But let us assume, in conforming with many classics of philosophical optimism, traditionally called dialectics, do I not have the right to assume that each ruin is truly a new becoming. Or at least something that does not allow this world to become petrified. Disintegration is the re-creation of the past into the future, someone who is more adept than me at creating aphorisms would have said.

I love flea markets, because for me these are like the visualized palpitation of life substances, the flowing across of the spiritual into the material and vice versa. This is the past, which seemingly once and for all has occurred, has exhausted itself, and seeks continuation for itself, thirsts further to be. Why these gas lamps, porcelain temple dancers, and family albums?

In the same way I love all kinds of family mythologies, at times intolerably confused and contradictory, accounts of trips, marriages, births, disappearances. I love the appearance in them of strange [foreign??] personages and unexpected offshoots. I even see how one morning over a century ago a Sudeten German by the name of Karl, for the first time in his life gets off a train at Stanislau Station – this is Galicia, he's never been here before, he only knows the fact that this is the most godforsaken hole in the entire country, a filthy province, to say it point-blank, simply the ass, the rear end, the Arsch, but right here he decides to begin life anew, *jawohl*, this is not his first (with strained interpretation a second) youth, he knows how to copy old paintings, he can paint icons for the Uniate Catholics, he's had a good Viennese schooling, he knows how to mix real colours, he knows nearly all the peculiarities of each kind of wood, every type of canvas, he's pedantic and respectable, he's masterful in his craft – this could become his daily bread – for him and his family, why not marry some Lutheran girl with a good dowry, time to find himself some kind of wife, don't you think, enough of gadding about impoverished villages. He has very few things with him, his entire previous life is contained in a tattered medium-sized travel bag (suspenders, underwear, a bowtie, a holiday vest, successfully acquired from the Krakow second-hand clothes seller Aron Gaier), somewhere close to the station he needs to find some kind of furnished rooms, preferably without fleas, but with breakfast; he decisively and somewhat suspiciously draws in air with his nose, striving to capture the first morning scents of the town.

And this was my great-grandfather. And here we abandon him, because this is just a single human story.

4
Exodus

Then there is my other great-grandfather – another line, another generation. He's five years old and three of those years he lived without his father, who went to America for work. The path that leads to America is the most direct path to the future. One could at least think about it that way. Each of us wants a better future for himself. When you get on the wrong side of forty, you usually stop thinking about your personal better future. Finally, after forty it stops making sense. You're thinking only about a better future for your children. The father of my great-grandfather used to think the same way. Children – that was his torment.

So, the future – it is in general a different continent, a kind of America, a New World, a clean sheet of paper. The future still remains the future, while you are floating, while the Great Water is around you, while the ship is swaying, while you're a fourth-class passenger, recruited by a headhunter company, and your face has turned blue from nausea. One wise ass has advised everyone just to look up from the deck at the sky under those circumstances – this apparently lessens the attacks of vomiting. I guess this, in essence, was just a metaphor. Or a tasteless joke.

The ship rocked back and forth amid the Great Water, fever struck children and grownups, dysentery squeezed it out of them, bodies of the dead were lowered overboard. The ocean fittingly accepted them as if they belonged to it.

America lay like a blank boundless meadow alive with angels, birds, and gold mines. Perhaps, too, like a diamond storehouse jam-packed with all kinds of stuff. Perhaps like a giant meat-packing plant, at which every day and night millions upon millions of dead bulls end up disembowelled. The father of my great-grandfather knew nothing more about America until the ship's eternity ended and it turned out that the ocean also had shores. Until the future stopped being the future.

However, at first he had to go through several weeks of a quarantine on one of the islands near the New York, Boston, or New Haven harbours. In time the administration began to confine itself to just mandatory sanitary processing in barracks especially set aside for that (looking into the mouth and ass, the rubbing of genitalia and underarms with some kind of stinking paste etc.), so that no Central-European, Jewish, Greek, Italian, Ruthenian, or Gypsy germ would not by chance penetrate the sterilely clean Land of Dreams. All this needed to be endured. The father of my great-grandfather had to endure this. Both the quarantine and the sanitary processing.

For some reason after a few years the letters from him stopped. His wife kept all his letters, she tied them with a ribbon into a single package. He wrote about how he was getting up at three in the morning for work, and how on Sunday he used to deny himself a second beer. Because he wanted to save a little money to return home and buy a piece of land. It was precisely this piece of land that now became his future. Land is always worth something. This is the only certainty, this land beneath your feet. Money loses value, palaces burn, and selected herds of cattle suddenly disappear beneath the land. But nothing would happen to the land – that is the firmest value. So he thought because he lived in the second half of the nineteenth century.

The land that he expected to buy was once supposed to have been divided among his children, it was to have been enough for everyone, it was supposed to have been a good-sized grain field, a territory of freedom and prosperity. This is how that future should have been.

But in truth his future turned out to be a tramcar, beneath the wheels of which he died in Chicago. In Russian about these kinds of victims they say "ego zarezalo tramvaem" (he was cut down by a streetcar). This is an impersonal form with the neuter "o" past-tense ending, the streetcar is only an implement of some ancient Greek doom. This is a blind catastrophe, lightning in a skull, the shrieks of demons, the screeching of braking tires on rails, sparks, instant horror, after which there is no pain, no sorrow.

His wife only found out about this standing over his grave. For a long time she had no letters from him, life became even more intolerable, caustic cousins hinted at infidelity (bordellos, cards, harems, and alcohol!); and a rich widower-neighbour had certain morganatic designs on her, but with money borrowed from her brothers and sisters (here in the middle of her story the entire tale about her running around and wheedling was squeezed in, about a world not without good people – a tale, pithily accomplished, about the saving grace of large and upright families); with the borrowed money she bought herself the same-class ticket for the very same company's ship. It is most interesting that she still returned – after nearly three decades, old and well-to-do (she was lucky, she worked as a seamstress twenty hours a day and by chance invested her money in the right bank). People no longer recognize her, she used a lot of strange words in her speech, she smoked strong tobacco, and from time to time allowed herself the pleasure of downing a shot. But all she yearned for – was to find her grown children, because now she could buy an abundance of land for each one of them.

Right before her trip to America, she parcelled her children out among several people who had enough food to feed them. Her children worked for the food; at that time it was the social norm, survival was the meaning of life, a bowl of broth was the meaning of a day survived. All her children, it seems, somehow survived, somehow provided for themselves and even during the first war none of them lost even a pinky. They ploughed through the next crisis of European humanism relatively painlessly, after all, they didn't have university degrees, and they read only from books about the Black Tulip and Fantômas, and never thought about things as complicated as the retreat from God, Oedipal complexes, or the twilight of Europe.

Somehow she could not find her youngest son (a fairytale! a fairytale!). He had been five years old when she ventured on her journey. He didn't want to live with strangers, he didn't want their bowl of broth for the sake of daily survival, he was, honestly, still too small to work at all, but big enough to run away from those strangers. The adults could have thought that he had run away for no particular reason, he ran away, for example from corporal punishment, from kneeling in the corner on shucked corn, from the stables, dung, pastures, from the master-of-the-house's snoring or the mistress's stench. In reality he had a plan, there was a grand idea with his own secret strategy for its fulfillment.

He went off into the world. Today everyone is capable of concocting something about this. About hiding under benches in trains and stage coaches, about night fears in boiler rooms and crates, about clothes torn by dogs and noses smashed in during fights, about the travelling circus, which he joined on the thirty-sixth day of his flight, the *salto mortale*, the swallowing of Bengal fires or subduing panthers – no, in reality just about washing the fecal deposits from under Peruvian llamas and a bald-pated dromedary, later about gypsies who taught him to understand pre-arranged signals and to beg, about Sunday kasha for the orphan children at a monastery. But the main thing was his movement, his journey along that patched together part of the world made of scraps, which in time would come to be called East Central Europe, and at that time (the end of the century, the fin de siècle, as Zarathustra would have put it) was still merely just a part of the most piecemeal of the most grotesque of empires. From scrap of land to scrap of land, from language to language, from landscape to landscape – that's the way he moved and that's how he found what he was looking for.

One day he ended up on the shore of a river. In his small and confined life he had not yet seen such wide rivers. More precisely – he didn't even discern it as a river. He just looked at the water, at the ship's fairway, at green islands and the distant shore. It happened that a certain rich and childless merchant had passed by him (the fairytale, the fairytale continues!). "At what are you lost in thought, little lad?" the merchant asked, bewildered perhaps by the adult intensity of that gaze. "I need to get to that shore," was the answer. "Why? Do you live there?" – "No, my mother is there. She's gone beyond the Big Water. And I've just found that Big Water. Now I have to find my mother beyond it."

You're in luck, the merchant answered that. I know where she is. She visits me sometimes. Come over to my house. The merchant had told a lie, but the story, in fact, ends here, because my great-grandfather believed him and from that day forward settled in his home. The merchant and his wife took him as a son and then even sent him to officer-training school. Why they chose to train him to be an officer, and not, say, a bird catcher, confectioner, or a priest, I don't know – it's unlikely it was out of patriotic passion with the premonition of world war. Or maybe they were refined, romantic people and had read the young writer Rilke: *Meine gute Mutter, seid stolz: Ich trage die Fahne?* . . .[5]

I also do not know how much of this fairytale is a fairytale. Family epics most often have a certain number of contradictory versions, not a single one of which also manages to jive with the official historical version of the sequence of events, which is known to us from textbooks. Besides this, family epics undergo the important influences of dime-store novels and TV serials, as a result of which any aunt Lutecia from the interwar twenty-year period suddenly plays the same pranks just like some exotic and exalted heroine out of a Paraguayan soap opera.

But I return to a picture that till this day appears to me. A small boy gazing over the river. Beyond the river the New World begins. America lies beyond the Danube, that is, the future, beyond the Danube lies everything that will come true (and not come true) in time. The Danube is really the Ocean, it draws. Its near presence means lots of things: time, eternity, history, mythology, us ourselves.

Yes, escapes – but also returns. Yes, the future – but also the past.

5
A Feuilleton

Free the future from the past?

Free the past from the future?

This sounds like the beginning of a poem. However, in my view, a poem overly theoretical, overly cold, and at the same time overly passionate. The single thing that saves this construction from a definitive lack of taste is the question marks at the end. It's good they are there.

Somehow for the umpteenth time I was present at the next in turn typical post-December-1991 meeting of Western intellectuals with those from the East. The conversation was about the resolution of many, as it seemed to them, extremely important things – about the "fall of the Wall and culture without borders," about the "coming together and opposition of mentalities," about "new nationalisms in old garments," about "the spiritual architecture of Europe in the third millennium," about "the post-carnival absurdities of the world." The discussions did not end up being too pointed, for such conferences "between East and West" in any one of the comfortable coffee-house cities of that *Mitteleuropa* generally do not get very heated – not a single spectre of the current political anti-heroes fails to disturb with its presence: neither Le Pen rushes on a steed with a speech, nor a Zhirinovsky with naked women and – a happening *a la Calachnikoff*, nor will Saddam Karadžič-Milošević read patriotic poetry, not a single evil genius, black swan, not a single bastard or fanatic, but mostly those nearly *of a single mind* gather, doctors of philosophy, philology, philanthropy, university universalists.

But here and there insignificant divergences surface, sorts of stumbling blocks. This is easy to explain by the many years (from time immemorial?) of existence in completely different systems, which, in fact, continues to this day. You can also explain this by all kinds of other walls and barriers of understanding, such as, for example, "Byzantine consciousness," "Protestant ethics," "post-colonial syndrome," "postmodernist exhaustion."

And there during that meeting one of the discussants (I believe from Sweden and himself a Swede) stated something like the following: "We don't have the need to know our history, because we never appeal to it. Happy societies have no need for history. Only unhappy societies absolutely need their history, for they yearn to explain their unhappiness to themselves and to others, to legitimize their failures, their incapability." I don't know whether he did this consciously or not, but it seemed to me that he really wanted to awaken the spirit of Nietzsche, but a Nietzsche quite vulgarized, a kind of *Nietzsche for the poor*.

Historiocentrism can be compared to phallocentrism, a certain woman colleague at another conference asserted. This is that vector, that shaft, that rod, which becomes the very essence of the world view of many intellectuals from the East. This is that cudgel, with which you eternally beat yourselves. Free your thinking from the dictate of history, finally make yourselves adequate for reality, she implored.

However, the *representatives of unhappy societies* contradicted her in such cases, but our unhappiness comes not from the fact that we thirst to enter deeply into a contemplation of our history. Here everything is, in fact, just to the contrary – we know it all too little, for in totalitarian times the history given to us was falsified, prepared, distilled, and burdened (therefore worn out), by "the single correct method." It all was completely transparent as a result of semantic emptiness, poor wretch, not only individual personages and events fell out from it, but even entire periods, tendencies, processes. Its content fell out from it. Thus we are now just beginning to reconstruct it, and this needs to happen.

You naive people, the *representatives of happy societies*, contradicted this, you naive people, you think now you will finally find another "single correct method" and will rid yourself of all problems thanks to a true explication of history. But the entire fact of the matter is that this is just an illusion, for history is just the sum of contradictory versions that really happened or in the same way did not happen in one or another dimension. In addition, historical vision never embraces all the complexity and fullness. Thus, history is falsified and reduced a priori and this is quite dangerous, but not less dangerous if you are conscious of this and know its, history's, place. History is masked mythology with a considerable – if not decisive – admixture of ideological necrophilia, and nothing more. It was precisely this love for history that gave birth to the scoundrels Il Duce and the Führer, for from where else but from these would have come these lictor bunches and runic signs, all these pompous Roman-Nordic paraphernalia with their caesars and siegfrieds? And finally, look at your own – already contemporary, already "non-totalitarian" (neo-totalitarian, yes!) school textbooks of history – look at what's written about your neighbouring nations? Look – and then later ask and be amazed, where hate comes from in this world and why till this day people are killed exclusively because they belong to this or that nation.

You'll never be able to understand us fully, certain historiocentric wretches replied to this. That organ with which you understand others has atrophied. Your supermarkets and six hundred and sixty-six TV channels have made you indifferent and self-satisfied. You won't end up well, Spengler was right.

And to you, the extra-historical fortunate people answered, it would be advisable for you first and foremost to rid yourself of your mentality. It remains totalitarian and this means that your short-lived democracies are under constant threat. Instead of a xenophobic rummaging about in the myths of history you'd be better off doing something about the mafia and corruption in your own countries. In such a situation you cannot count on the prospect of joining "Inner Europe" with its liberally cosmopolitan and consumptively hedonistic values. Thus you're only blindly finishing laying bricks for a wall that, it would seem – we had come to an agreement! – must be knocked down.

So in mutual intimidation, somewhat fruitful discussions passed, although everything ended, as a rule, with reconciliation: from the moderators a saving idea emerged regarding terminological disagreement, the inaccuracies in synchronic translations, the necessity to come to an understanding *in bad English*, and finally, one of the oldest, who didn't catch anything, began to try to convince everyone of the right to his or her own manner of seeing, and of the diversity of opinions as the intellectual richness of the world.

About the concluding banquet, I'll just say that during it – everything was settled definitively.

There was, true, a certain radical from Moscow, who imagined himself to be a dog and tried to nip at the calves of Western women. This was a part of his conception about the futility of all spiritual efforts and about the impossibility of understanding between the East and the West. The police did not intervene, in fact, and they weren't even there. What would the police be doing there where the topic is liberation?

6
A Compendium

So what can you do with this emancipation? Of the past? Of the future? Where can we lay out among them this mostly unwise creature inclined to self-deceptions with its pretenses and instincts, this *sweet child in time*?

Borges, slowly sinking into darkness, said that there are only four human stories. Human visions of the past and future are even fewer. It seems there are only two. But our self-consciousness begins from them. Actually, the person who formulated *"To hope is human"* can be noted as the first. There are thousands of definitions of a human, let there be one like this – a two-legged creature without feathers, whose property is hope.

The first of two visions of a human in time is more profound, for it arises from the primordial child's plasma of *homo sapiens* and is protected and directed by the will to live. Concordant with this, the past becomes like one "suffered through hell," and the future like "an anticipated paradise." That is, it's worth it that we live for the sake of changes for the better, and all the changes are for the better. The past swallows our imperfection, our mistakes, downfalls, tragedies; wounds and pain remain in the past. There is no such pain that does not pass. There is no such wound that does not heal. There is no such suffering that is impossible to endure or such a loss that you cannot suffer through, says Yogi Ramacharaka.[6] Insofar as the main sense of existence is suffering, then the appropriation of time lies in this swallowing of it by the past.

(Here is a passing recollection from the poet Volodymyr Svidzynsky: "Who will tell me into which abysses/Into which time will sink?" But even non-poets well know something about this special sense of poets.)

On this opposition of the past "hell" and the future "paradise," all utopias have sprouted without exception, so we also can accept it as *utopian*. Viewed in such a way, the future is an unconditional synonym of the "better," the future demands no apologetics, which is undoubtedly present in it, the way the existence of God is present in crystals of salt. It is precisely from this – all innovations without exception originate, improvements, the German *Erfindungsgeist*, technical and social progress, beautiful gestures of the merry-makers of humankind, the great geographic discoveries. I do not doubt the existence of the most complex cultural plots worked out in detail about the path from Columbus to Campanella and vice versa: great communist America dragged into the infinity of its golden future the part of Western (and not just Western) humanity most thirsting for *changes for the better*. It is precisely from here – stuck in my childhood memories, the old Soviet hit song about apple trees that will bloom on Mars as well as Marx's maxim that all of pre-Marxian history of humanity is only pre-history, and true history begins in fact from now, that is, with Marx's teachings.

Hence also – all revolutions without exception, including the velvet and the sexual one, the sex-appealing Freedom on the barricades of 1848 and – even more so – 1968, night tribunals, the victorious spasms of the consumptive commissar-apostles, and the bulging eyes on the lopped off heads of monarchs. Hence – the gymnastically springy gait of Marinetti, and also a demolition charge placed beneath the museums of the world. Hence – all of avant-gardism, this variety of terrorism in art, all its black squares; hence comes terrorism itself, terrorism as such, a solely human form of inclination before an idea, idealism squared, the last refuge of iron knighthood, guided on the radio by the Highest

Necessity. Hence the idea of the Millennial Reich with the yellow waves of the Indian Ocean that crash on its ancient Aryan shores in the final vision just before the death of a teenager from the *Hitlerjugend* with grenades latched all over his body. Hence the impertinent idea of light at the end of a tunnel, with which so obstinately and blindly millions of subjects of One-Sixth[7] of the world overcame misery, dirt, the abyss of communist cells, around-the-clock lines for soap and buckwheat groats, and a Chekist crushing genitals during interrogations. Hence, also the hedonistic idea of a New Europe, a kind of recreational rose garden, an eternally green park without borders and conflicts, where everyone is meek, well-off, and tolerant, where everyone additionally is already nearly immortal, where each has found him- or herself a place by his or her own millennial yew-tree – and solemnly hums a well-known text by Schiller to a Beethoven motif.

The second vision, certainly, has a later origin – for it to appear a sinful fall had to occur, a consciousness of a world that incessantly collapses into evil had to come. Here the past arises as an unconditional positive, the past as a "paradise lost." Instead, the future is like "the end of the world," a universal catastrophe, the last reckoning with evil before some kind of other, non-human, qualitatively higher existence. In this way I've ventured to name this opposition of the past and future *apocalyptic*, although the real scope of its deep-laid etymology and semantics is, in fact, considerably wider than properly Christian doctrine.

However, precisely in this context there is the well-known inscription read off an Egyptian papyrus about social decay, about dreadful young people, who hold nothing sacred, about universal decay and licentiousness, the collapse of a positive world view, epidemics of incurable diseases, raids of cannibalistic tribes from the desert, and the catastrophic drop in the water level of the Nile. As a result of all these mentioned and unmentioned factors, "this world will soon come to an end." (After five thousand years we are amused by this prophecy of a hypochondriac scribe-analyst, we perceive it as a curious example of a tedious, moralizing self-assuredness or a *primitive fixation on the social*, without wondering even a bit at the same time what exactly did its author have in mind when he said "soon": maybe that's exactly five thousand years?)

Hence the parabolas of a past "golden age" and a paradisal garden with the chirping of exotic birds (now extinct), and the "childhood of humankind" with its pre-initiation, pre-sinful purity, and the Vedic degradation of the material world from "gold" to "iron," a gradual degradation of essences, an inexorable falling of darkness.

Right in this system of notions abide not only the four horsemen and the trumpets of the angels, but entire epochs of a "final premonition" with persistently manifested "chronological paranoia," when already the very date – the ordinal number of the year – testifies to the end of ages: 666! 1313! 1500! 1998! 2000!!!

Here, amid this version of the world, are the visions of Bosch, nurtured by the Adamites, and all the other visions and self-immolations of sectarians, and English graveyard metaphysics with an obligatory Triumphal Worm in the end, and Calderón's assertion that "life is a dream," and *Weltschmerz*, and Edgar Allan (born as Edgar Poe) buried alive with his *nevermore*, and Charles Baudelaire, a smoker of opium, and Ludwig II of Bavaria with his insatiable inclination for Wagner, and the drunken Rimbaud on a ship, and all the other flowerings of decadence, including the polygamous orgies in towers and cellars, the fashion for incest, and the mass suicides of high school students disillusioned by the routine of existence.

But here, quite nearby, are also millions of recent subjects of the One-Sixth, for whom, it turns out, paradise was taken away. And with it, evidently, memory too – they so easily forgot about the misery, the grime, the abyss of communist cells, around-the-clock lines for soap and buckwheat groats, the crushing of genitalia at interrogations, they forgot about the predetermined grey boredom of existence, about control over souls, about a deficit of condoms and the lifetime wait for a "cage for reproduction" known as an apartment, about hundreds of hundreds of *temporary shortcomings*. Instead they remember something quite the opposite: inexpensive bread, free and self-sacrificing physicians (not necessarily poisoners), *a life without dollars, the mafia, and sex*, equality in poverty, evening invitations to neighbours to watch black and white TV, mineral spring health spas in the Crimea and Caucasus, hockey victories over Canadian professionals, international crossbreedings in Soviet-wide construction projects, the songs of Lyudmila Zykina or Sophia Rotaru, the appearance in stores on May Day of "Soviet Champagne," albeit fleeting like a shower on the first of May. The majority of them recall their youth – not more, but not less. There were also hundreds of hundreds of other *advantages*, because we're talking here in general about a person's youth – nothing more, nothing less.

Thus in this eternally transitory *zone*, in this so anachronistic *single cultural space*, through which with eternal lateness, but all the same in the end the Ammensdorf *soft* first-class train cars roll along, marked with the stamp *Vereinigter Schienenfahrzeugbau der Deutschen Demokratischen*

Republik (perhaps all that's left of the East German utopia, besides the yet unexposed agents of the Stasi, and not even those have remained!), in these fields between Europe and Noneurope, we discover millions of people with a "stolen paradise," lost people, angry, weary, their love for the past grows over everything, this particular variant of former ones. They already don't need any kind of future. The future is a black hole, it's a daily increase in prices for ritual funeral services, that's what the future looks like. And if they have certain expectations, then it's exclusively for the past. More accurately, for the possibility of a complete restoration of the past in the near future. For the sake of this they go to elections and vote. This, it seems, is how an "apocalyptic" vision for a short time again transforms into a "utopian" one – but in truth you can't restore anything, you can't drive out *dollars* or the *mafia* from our life, like *sex* either. But how do you explain to them that even our society hewn with stone axes, is a considerably more complicated edifice than even the cathedral at Chartres; that is why restoration is impossible and there will be no sharing of champagne or spas as there will not be equality, brotherhood (at least of *those, their*), and a new historical society (at least *this* one)? And there will just be the wearying floundering of politicians, confusion, stamping in place, and a vicious circle of those same causes and results, a circle so vicious that you'll never manage to differentiate them – which are the causes, and which are the results.

This is the past that hinders the realization of the future. A past that holds it in its clutches. A past as the dictate of preconception.

7
Epitaph

A silver ring with the initials *M.A.*, several photographs, and the last phrase before death, personally speaking, is all that remained for me from my grandfather. The past goes before us, it strives to warn us about something, sometimes it does succeed.

I never saw my grandfather alive, because death came to him sixteen years before my birth. We missed each other in massifs of time, and if it's true that on the other side each time new and newer procedures await us, then right now it already is harder and harder to say who of us belongs more to the past – he or I.

I never saw him alive? In reality I only see him alive. The eldest of five brothers and sisters and therefore quite solitary among them; quite early he fled from home so as to experience all the enticements of sitting in typhus-laden trenches. He loved being a military man, but for his entire life he succeeded in doing that just twice – in 1918 and in the 1940s. He followed a sufficiently clear, but, as it turned out, not sufficiently pragmatic, religion: one entitled the *emancipation of his homeland*. Ukraine was one, but her enemies were both the Poles and the Soviets. At a suitable moment it was necessary to raise up arms against them. Even the devil himself could have set forth in this matter, that completely was in agreement with his, grandfather's, sceptical sense of humour and nearly atheistic convictions of a person of the *lost generation*, who still in his youth managed to see human extremities ripped apart by shells. He waited for the proper moment for an entire twenty years – half of his life. All this time (while the manifestos of the surrealists were being written, and silent movies learned to speak in human voices), he spent time playing cards, listening to the radio, with strolls in the mountains – on horseback, skis, and on foot, hunting, automatic billiards, crosswords, flirting, and short but stormy returns to his family life. The war again in fact separated him from his wife and children (was he happy about that opportunity?), though sometimes they saw each other in Stanislav. His diabolical accomplice failed the war little by little, but he, like thousands of *optimists* similar to him, didn't stop nurturing their hope that as a result of a final conflict of a brown Satan with a red one, they would succeed in achieving the *emancipation of their land*.

All this ends in the spring of 1944, in a train of evacuated Ukrainians that is moving to the southwest somewhere between Kamyanka-Buzka and Lviv. In Lviv, new battle-ready units were supposed to be formed for repulsing the Soviets (they were striving all the time to do that!). The uniforms had been sewn, the use of carbines permitted, the songs penned – onward, falcon-soldiers!

But he didn't make it to Lviv. In the sky over the troop transport train the planes of the Red Army appeared. My grandfather had just finished smoking his cigarette when the bombing and the firing at the wagons began from above. Besides the turmoil, the flashes, explosions, and the hot crackling of the thirteen-millimetre bullets ripping the train car's panel walls, he stepped over to the window – to throw out his unfinished cigarette butt, or to evaluate the situation. Finally his rank and experience laid on him the responsibility to give out some kinds of commands. He opened the window and even leaned through it – it was as though in the underground training camps the old Galician master sergeants didn't teach him to be cautious and first and foremost hide his head from the bullets. The planes passed by really low, in *shaving flight* – it seems that's what it's called. At that instant some lieutenant, well, say his name is Ivanenko, born in the Poltava, Sumy, or Kherson region, the only member of his family who survived the great famine, a Komsomol member and a candidate to be an aerial ace, went into a dive. The speed of the plane is faster than the speed of the braking train, better to shoot short bursts.

My grandfather already saw the shadow of that wing above him. "Commander, sir, be careful, get back from the windows!" An orderly began to bellow at him (he will later bring the silver *M.A.* ring and this story). "Like hell they'll get me," my grandfather said in a steady voice, after which he fell, rent by a machine-gun round. The cigarette-box in his breast pocket over his heart didn't help at all.

In this life my grandfather had everything he desired – two wars, several girlfriends, a family, children, mountain landscapes, and sudden death from the sky. Besides that, he was a good shooter and horseback rider. He told jokes that were mostly dirty and salty. His love for obscenities sometimes is echoed in me – right at those moments I find the most necessary formula for coming to an understanding with the world.

His life wasn't all that bad, crowned with a final military man's joke. And not a single one of his words was lost – they were heard even in the roar of an aerial attack.

More than anything I love these last words of his. I repeat them each time I'm attacked. It's easier for me from them. I sense behind me Someone Big, His now otherworldly strength and support. Like hell they'll get me – I repeat to myself, and it always helps. It's almost like the silver ring – a protective circle, we are connected through it, we aren't alone.

8
Meditation

Oh, if only someone could free this world from the past! To attain lightness, unfetteredness, purity, to find amnesty in amnesia! One wants so badly to add one's voice to the numerous futurophile proclamations and happenings, especially right now at the instant when it's not far at all to the future.

But on the other hand, you can't punish the guilty eternally. Even more so, if he is already defenceless. Is the dictatorship of the future any less wearisome? Is the future with its cynical logic of *changes for the better* not interfering in our gestures, intentions, hopes, and actions? Is it not with all the unceremoniousness of something unconditionally great, powerful, and larger than us, swallowing everything? In due time I sometimes met people, who assert, as though it, the future, is the only reality in the world. One of them in his time had excavated ten or so burials in the lowlands of the Don, and today hides from the Moscow passport control regulations in the abysses of a meditative trance in the kitchens of his friends, it seems, suspected of terrorism. "See," said the excavator of burials, having fallen in spirit for a short time from some lotus-covered extraterrestrial dales to the eight square metres of a kitchen, where in the meantime his own body patiently waited and asked for vodka, unconscious, self-hypnotized, tattered by *samsara*, and abandoned there on a rug; "see, everything that once happened and now is happening, smeared in the space Moment – everything has taken place and is taking place exclusively sanctioned by the future. I saw *from there*. The past, no matter how we might understand it, is merely an unsuccessful projection of the future, its always imperfect imitation. Most often – its feeble victim. If you were to put gigantic amounts of money into this question, you could create an Institute of the Future. I'm planning on writing up proposals and sending them to all the existing foundations and centers." (After these words once again he flew off somewhere, that is, his body remained with a glass of Komdyv[8] vodka in his hands, but his spirit decisively flew off *to beyond the boundaries* – maybe at that Moment thoroughly combing through the offices of some extraterrestrial Lotus Foundations and Centres.)

I would say to this that the intrusion of the future is always an inescapable catastrophe, because the opened bottle of Komdyv *was disposed towards agreement*, but I never said any such thing as a result of my ingrained hate of the categorical. For in this case we must agree with the fact that existence is catastrophic in general, but in no way did it look that way in this kitchen cage, at three in the morning, among countless cigarettes and a drinking spree. Thus why must we agree with that? Is it not in our nature to look for an alternative? Why is doom just left to us, this being eternally torn between these two monsters, between these imagined chimeras, between the unknown "once" that no longer is, because it already happened, and yet one more unknown "once," that still has yet to be, because it still has not happened? In reality, both the past and the future are somehow situated beyond the boundary of our attainability. We are neither there nor there. These are abysses, each one of which scrutinizes us with scorn and examination. Or maybe it is we who are gazing into abysses (as they wrote in Gothic novels, *unable to turn away their gaze*)? How can we find the strength within us to turn away from them?

How can we free the present, that is the question I would be emboldened to call in the highest measure kitchen and philosophical one. Our "now" is the only thing that we have in reality. If a certain philosophical incorrectness has crept in here in a front of Existence, I'll emend myself: "now" is the one place where we in reality are, to which we in reality belong. (To have? To be? To belong? I surmise this is terribly close, maybe just a difference in words.) But the know-how to recognize "now" – this, perhaps, is the only path to come to an understanding of our surroundings. "Now" is the one thing for which we are accountable. Because at least this is no chimera, this is, this is right now, this is with us. Here it is, here it is, here it is slipping out . . .

Obviously, the poets were the first to talk about this with their own synthetic feminine sensitivity. (Spring ruins poets in the same way like it does women: the skin blossoms, the mucous membrane is irritated to exhaustion, an allergy to scents compels to sensitivity, tears in the eyes, sticky spots instead of objects and a complete spatial disorientation.) Any kind of lyric poetry is always "now," this abiding not "between," but "inside," and abiding "inside" is always loftier, more grateful, and more noble, for it designates your connectedness, your being involved, your presence – in difference from a separated, torn away, and abandoned abiding "between."

Right from here – easily recognized by its spoiled, capricious childhood, the outrageous and doomed to a failure pretension of a certain Weimar doctor of the Middle Ages, an old sorcerer and skirt-chaser: *verweile̲ doch, du bist so schön!* After all, this transport of joy does not belong at all to philosophy, this is not the subject of reflections and the trained from rostra and stages mind's habit to the provocation of abstractions, this rather is the effect of presence, the effect of the moment, the effect of presence in life, this is life itself, its swaying and fluttering, and it is precisely this – irrespective of the aphoristic gift of the Weimar seducer – that any one of us, the unenlightened, is ready to exhale at any time, to moan (the beauty of the body, of the summer, a landscape, the taste of biscuits, the scent of ruins, so that anything at all burst forth from us, for the possibilities for love are, fortunately, countless, and the possibilities for feeling it – even more).

Somehow, wandering about in distress in the dense, inaccessible estates of Eliot near Burnt Norton, I have struck against the same thing (the devil take it, that culture with all its reminiscences!):

Time past and time future
What might have been and what has been
Point to one end, which is always present.

Though, why have I observed the "same thing?" Yes, Eliot seemingly placed the "here and now" above all other fictions, and seemingly acknowledged that however we name "everything else," it only leads, it only brings, it only serves, it only sets off.

It is the now that is absolute. But why is there the *"end"*? The completion of time? The here and now as the final concentration of illusoriness? *The here and now as never*? Is the final and ghastly stop of this still "Weimarian" instant embodied in the next suicide of lyric energy?

I don't always have the opportunity to look for commentaries or to dive into Augustine or even Proust. I am left to ponder time, relying on my personal experiences. I would have understood immeasurably more if I had managed to read ten times more wise books and – even more important – if I had managed to remember them. In the meantime the same things happen to me that happen with everyone: I live in time, I live time, I pass in it. And there is left for me at least to make use of it in my striving to speak about changes, losses, abysses. Soon I will be forty years old, so I've achieved a minimal right to this. It has all begun: a new count, life after year 2000, part two (sadder), that very same novel in which a different hero suddenly appears, that very same series in which the hero is now played by a different actor, a further quickening rush downward, the flickering of hospitals, hospices, a greater frequency of funerals that you should attend, unmotivated alcoholic breakouts in the direction of a parallel reality, quivering and frenzy, tachycardia, oxygen starvation, and finally fear as such.

Just now have I begun learning to love the present. But twenty years ago (people don't live that long!) with my head, with my arms, and with my legs I was devoted to the future, above all I loved the future and loved it as much as I loved myself. I even terribly wanted this future to come as quickly as possible, so that time, as they got used to saying about it, really would fly – I was sure approximately of the same thing that, it seems, Epicurus assured himself: "While we live, there is no death, and when death comes, we no longer are." I, of course, could not formulate this with the same roguish brilliance. Surely my not fully formed sentience would sound less convincing, but on the other hand with more frankness: "Why should we put off the future? Why fear it? For it is our eternal renewal, our new possibilities, new banquets of reality. For example, new women, poetry, journeys, masks. And regarding our new losses, that is why they are losses, for us to go beyond the borders of time, beyond the borders of the future, beyond the borders of us, that is, not to be concerned with us. Yes, losses don't concern us."

This is sufficiently mixed up and doubtful. It would be better simply to be filled with joy, to drink wine at the ruins of castles, and repeat following Epicurus like an incantation: "While we are alive. While we are alive."

9
Bildungsroman

While his father was alive, my father knew that a giant was standing over him. He lived his teenage life, went to school at the gymnasium where he was taught Latin, got into street fights with the *Volksdeutsch*[9] and in his copy books drew the first girls, who looked like Marika Rökk[10] the movie star. In the spring of forty-four, when grandfather's orderly brought him a silver ring and a cigarette case, for the first time in his life he felt cold from the touch of true male loneliness. His sister had perished in the Dnister River last year. Mother barely survived that, and here – the death of her husband. At fourteen years of age my father suddenly came to understand that he is responsible.

The Russians were advancing, they were told from everywhere, you need to pack up your belongings. The front line really and inexorably began to crawl from the East. The Russians were advancing. What this meant, to them, the witnesses of the blocked with human bodies prisons and cellars; there was no need to explain. (*The last days of June of forty-one, a strange time between the Russians and the Germans, shirts sticky from sweat, the stench of corpses on the main street of the city, go to identify your dead.*)

Existence between the Russians and the Germans is the historical destiny of Central Europe. The Central European fear historically sways between two anxieties: the

Germans are advancing, the Russians are advancing. Central European death – this is a prison or concentration camp death, a collective one too, *Massenmord, a purge*. The Central European journey – this is escape. But from and to where? From the Germans or the Russians? It's good that there still is American America for these instances in the world.

My father actualized his Central European journey in forty-four and forty-five. Again, this was a train, this time the train of refugees, an entire transport train of all kinds of humanity, traditionally called the Galician intelligentsia – engineers, physicians, lawyers, the gymnasium *professorate*, editors of newspapers, caricature politicians, and trade union swindlers – all of them with their womenfolk (activists, unionists from the Union of Ukrainian Women and from Prosvita-Union, children, servants and domestic creatures, especially cats; the transport train occasionally contained several independent theatres with all the ethnographic requisites, several libraries, archives, museums, a printing office, a capella of bandurists together with banduras, a mixed church choir, and finally, even a portable church, as well as a lot of other things. This was in general a perfect bedlam with its internal war for survival, its intrigues, adulterers, and *mésalliances*. The train moved awfully slowly, stopped for a long time in some fields or deserted stations, made some loops and detours unmotivated by anything, feeding mostly on rumours and fears: the Russians are advancing. But this time they obligatorily will stop them on the Kovel–Brody–Ternopil line, professional optimists assured them with secret certificates hidden in their breast pockets.

All of this was movement towards the West, and in it there also was present that saddest accidental pair – a mother and son, a fragment of a once happy family past, Christmas Eve dinners, and mountain bicycle trips with all the four of them, a fragment of happiness, with the crackling of the grindings by the machine of life. (He remembered how long and persistently he tried to convince her of the necessity to go, to escape, to slip away, as she didn't understand the arguments directed at her about some kind of threat there (*how could there be any threats after all that had happened?*), as for lengthy moments she stood still, as though she were listening to something completely her own; as each time she smoked the next cigarette, a strong men's type of cigarette; as later she collected some things completely automatically, losing the thread of common sense (*and why he is alive, how can he be alive when they're already gone?*), forgetting the most practical, instead she remembered first and foremost just: the ring, the cigarette case, several locks of her daughter's hair, cut off before she was placed in the coffin.)

After Lviv the train rode for an intolerably long time to Przemysl, where tens of families joined it, among them all her sisters and brother, an entire brood of sympathy and pity, but why was there all this feigned grief? "Poor Irena," they said, "poor Irena." Although the death of her husband in their eyes seemed completely logical – he himself had wanted it. Clearly, they hadn't loved him enough during his life, especially for his mocking humour. He had mocked himself into a mess, they wagged their heads, with suspicion looking closely at his son – the boy showed some of the worst of his father's features: he spoke not overly politely, avoided company, quite often would seclude himself ("Might he be masturbating, Irena?"), and several times was caught red-handed smoking.

In the meantime the train directly rode into May, which that year was mostly rainy and cold; after Krakow the train for some reason moved its way not towards Vienna, but to the south, and finally stopped in the mountains for several months, amid the sycamore maple forests covered with the first green. Everyone was allowed to be busy with their own affairs: jurists juried, healers healed, engineers, editors, politicians – all of them somehow recovered, played cards, divided up in new abodes, the theatre had the opportunity to recreate *Matchmaking in Honcharivka* and to start rehearsals of *Where the Feather Grass Rustled*; the printing office also made some noise, multiplying appeals of female unionists regarding the temporary occupation of Ukraine and the prevention of syphilis. Even the gymnasium teachers found use for themselves, unexpectedly resuming the school year; and my father pretended as if he were continuing his study of Latin, every day driving from Żegiestów to Krynica with several of the guys his age. After the end of classes, there was a free hour before the departure of the local train, and each time he would give up his change saved at the school breakfast for the opportunity to go up the legendary Krynica funicular, the iron horse of the Polish tourist business. (Mineral springs, picturesque neighbourhoods, and the higher Warsaw world including cavalry general officers, geniuses of the Polish secret service called *defenzywa* and Opera Orpheuses – he remembered all of this from the 1930s from illustrated magazines of movie newsreels.) Then he for a time remained on the mountain, gazing at the slopes, at the forests, at the rooftops of the little town below, at all of Lemko Land, training himself to recognize the surrounding mountaintops – Yavoryna? Magura? – always solitary always incomprehensible ("Is he maybe hiding something, Irena?"). The local train appeared from the direction of

Muszyna and, until it made its way crawling to the station, and then started to move towards Piwniczna, my father managed to run down and get on the last train car, just so as not to ride with everyone.

He really did conceal things – first and foremost his catastrophic lagging behind in age. He had just turned fifteen, the time was sticky and awfully leisured, though in a month the trumpets trumpeted for them again – the Russians were advancing. It turns out that the front in the East was broken next, and they had to pack up again and escape, so far as possible from this Ukraine, may bright lightning strike her with all her invisible heroes.

Thus that same train again was replenished with refugees (the number of lawyers and swindlers increased, the mixed church choir became truly mixed, a single indivisible family, in as much as in the meantime everyone in it managed to sleep with everyone else, though judging by external appearance it wasn't given away). The yellow certificates of the refugees guaranteed care and support. Some, in fact, disappeared forever in the labyrinths of the Gestapo: a stone thrown into a river. Such was the fate of those eternally suspicious Galicians – the Russians were destroying them for collaborating with the Germans, and the Germans – for collaborating with the Russians. Besides that, some of the sickest ones remained forever in this mountainous place of healing, in its bowels, its ground, closer to its mineral springs.

But the train moved further along, although it was perhaps a different train. Further there was Slovakia, the quintessence of the Centre and Europe, a land of allies, and finally, at that time a liquidated satellite formation with a priest-president at its head. They crossed countless tunnels and bridges above tempestuous waters; on both sides there were still the mountains, inexpressibly tasty names of stations, cities, and towns sand deeply into memory and with the same lightness were blown from it: Stará Ľubovňa, Liptovský Mikuláš, Kežmarok, Poprad, Žilina, Púchov (the transport train moved further on and it unforeseenly seemed like the Berlin strategists, to whom it undoubtedly was subordinated, themselves don't know what to do with it further and thus they had to improvise incessantly, trying to mix up the Russian SMERSH,[11] Red Slovaks, and the intelligence service. So to such an extent all these amateur theatres turned out to be important for them. Among the refugees two main versions were circulated: according to the first (the realistic one), the train was to arrive in Vienna, after which everyone would be forced to be relocated throughout the Reich, each with some different aim, however it is well-known that *jedem das seine;*[12]

according to the second (fantastic one), the train long ago had been ruled by no one and directed nowhere – by inertia some kind of railroad demons were dragging it forward, and some otherworldly forces had already set up for it an appropriate black tunnel, that had to end with an eternal abyss, though, in this case, that same inevitable *jedem das seine* was foreseen.

At times ruined castles appeared on the mountain peaks – my father gazed into these fragments of former plenitude with the frenzied ardour of a nomadic warrior. Sometimes, during one of the next of incomprehensible stops, he made his way to a large natural castle setting for a hike. There he could contemplate and observe, underground inhabitants forged swords for him, he put a *surma*[13] up to his lips and from Gerlach Peak he summoned flying armies. His aunts energetically attacked him after every time he returned ("He's growing up a bit wild, Irena!"). Let him be, she said, he's painting, like our father, and writing short stories, he'll be an artist.

The small town in which they stopped closer to winter was called Holíč and lay on an imaginary border with Moravia. Attempts at a settled life began again, first and foremost theatre rehearsals. My father was invited to play the role of some kind of orderly in a Kozak production – and, though he had all of two quick-as-lightning entrances on stage, but nevertheless in one of them he was supposed to swordfight with a wooden sabre. However, his main achievement was soccer. One Sunday afternoon local players called onto the field a solitary observer-foreigner. He showed himself to be the best, scored several goals, and towards the end of the match – these kinds of days happen! – he substituted for the goalie and also knocked away a penalty shot. They immediately offered him a place on the first team of the Holíč Football Club and in a week he had already stepped onto the field in a red with black stripes jersey for a match in the Slovak league against "Union" from Skalica. The match turned out to have been really brutal, there were mostly older guys on the first team of the "Union" team, massive bulls, mostly policemen and firemen. Over the course of the entire match they repeatedly stepped on his feet, one time even on his neck, but he hit his goal sometime in the second half when the persecutor rivals already, as they say, were toast (yesterday's slivovitz had worried them to death). He stepped off the field limping awfully, but to an ovation that was his five minutes of fame – for the first and last time in his life he had an ovation. The FC Holíč coach, the owner of the local bakery and a little bit of a cranky Slavophile, pressed his palm and with a tear in his eye announced that from that moment on – he would be on his team for keeps.

But at that moment no one yet knew that in two days the train of *displaced persons* would be moving further: the Russians again were approaching, their chief had given them just a few weeks to end this entire war, the enemy needed to be finished off in its own lair in *Wolfschanze* immediately, the situation would not tolerate any procrastination. Central Europe demanded emancipation, the pearls of culture were mined, brotherly peoples through the voices of Moscow radio stations howled about salvation, it was clear to everyone that the Germans, for the second time in this century, would get squashed. It was also actually unknown for what reason they chased this entire train to Vienna and ordered everyone to get off there with their things – right at the Wien-Nord station, where they later spent several days and nights waiting for further orders, from time to time running into bomb shelters before air attacks, together with hundreds of other similar-to-them homeless refugees from the East and from the Balkans with all kinds of *traitors to the homeland, with Nazi sycophants*, provocateurs, agents of the Cheka, old UNR[14] emigrants, broken pieces of some other Ukraine, women, children, and all manner of riffraff.

("Be sure to go on the *Riesenrad*[15] in Prater Park," my father advised me right before my departure for Vienna. This was the only thing that astounded him from the half-ruined Danube capital – the "devil's wheel" (as we call it in Ukrainian), the Riesenrad in Prater Park; all the same he had taken a ride on it; he all the same had seen the Danube and *Stefansdom*, and the city hall, and *Votivkirche*, and the smoky city gaping with cavities from the height nearly of a bombardier; he really managed to do that: the allies (or was it maybe the Bolsheviks?) bombed the park and completely destroyed the Ferris wheel just several days later; also, as everything else in the German-speaking part of the world, that time the emptied attractions still functioned punctually, despite the war and the general *humanitarian catastrophe*. "Be sure to go on the *Riesenrad*," he repeated to me after fifty odd years, already without getting up from his bed; I had come to say good-bye before my departure, but why for Pete's sake should I in my thirty-seventh year need to see this shitty *Riesenrad*, I wanted to answer, though, thank God, I remained silent. Well, my father's enthusiasm for all kinds of oddities demanded from me somewhat of a more attentive view: wandering menageries, zoos, serpentaria, motorcycle races along a vertical surface, exhibits of Wolf Messing or the Chinese circus from the early times of Mao Zedong invariably gushed out in his narrations, like the funicular in Krynica and – a special case! – the Translucent Person, a movable exhibit made of glass, brought to Stanislav at the time of the Germans occupation, a work of Prussian discipline of thought and of a naturalist genius, irreplaceable for the study of human anatomy, through a glass surface of the body one could follow the arrangement and work of the plaster cast internal organs, the flow of blood, the secretion of bile, of the gastric juices, lymph, saliva, sperm, all this was highlighted in appropriate colours, was in unceasing movement and interacted; this lasted a good two weeks, and my father nearly every day went to look at that; later this Transparent Man was packed up into a special case and by special train transported further, probably somewhere towards Zalishchyky–Ternopil.)

The allies bombed the Wien-Nord train station the next night after my father and mother had gotten off it (death again was unable to catch the right beat). Regarding them finally a decision of unknown and panicked Berlin strategists came to a head: together with all relatives and several tens of other refugees after two weeks of plotting in the barracks in a giant camp near Vienna they were directed deep into Austria and resettled in some Sitzgrass[16] or some other such village with a similar name (you won't find it on any map; I looked and know what I'm talking about but all the same I see this Sitzgrass in all its typicality: the Gothic architecture of the church, a clock on a tower, a narrow street with a post office and wine shop, the cooing of pigeons, an old baron's estate on a hill – *ein Schlößchen*, an alley of chestnut trees, the Alps on the horizon, a water mill, and swimming in greenish water. Because it simply can't be any other way!). And while the war was ending, while the last of the last blond rogues were giving up their lives for the Thousand-Year Reich from the Atlantic to the Indian Ocean including Transylvania and Scythia, until the Austrians declared that they after all are Austrians, and not Nazis at all, until all this was happening, spring was gathering in strength everywhere, my father was finishing up the last of his lectures of a dead language, as well as some other languages. Later summer began, the American administration still didn't know what they should do with these so-called *Displaced Persons*, but in the meantime nourished them with salted nuts, canned beer, and densely packed stubby cigarettes with a camel and pyramid on a yellow pack. "It's utter happiness it's the Americans," his aunts repeated, "it's utter happiness it's not the Bolsheviks," they further clarified their thought. Each one of them knew how to set out tens of different kinds of playing cards, and father remembered several of them: "Red and Black," "Solitaire," and "Portrait Gallery." Sometimes he disappeared for a long time in the surrounding forests, just nationalized after the baron, and no one now will ever find out how things were with him that summer, with whom he met up with – under the roof of a hunting cabin, under a thousand-year-old yew tree, under the gun sight of the Yankee guard, under every bush, and no one will find out how many times and what her name was . . .

"I'm sorry," the lady *officer* said to his mother at the beginning of autumn. She was a person with a rather unfeminine dry skin and voice, *"I'm sorry, but you have to return home. With your son,"* she added, so as not to leave any doubts, and then repeated all this in imperfect Polish. This was nothing other than the execution of allied obligations before pockmarked Josef – to give back to Moscow all its former subjects. This was called the lovely word "repatriation," because the Latin patria means fatherland, and he remembered this, like the byword expression *dulce et decorum est pro patria mori*,[17] that he was forced once to write one hundred and fifty times in his school copybook on the order of nasty and pedantic professor Chaikovsky.

No one, besides the two of them, not a single of mother's sisters together with all their relatives was not subject to this return home, in as much as not one of them for a single minute had been a citizen of One-Sixth [of the world]. In this way they were viewed like a part of the West, citizens of the free world, however – they had to remain in this free world. "Poor Irena," her sisters said, "what's waiting for her there?" Some started talking about escape, about making fake documents, about destroying an old certificate, about a name change; someone even suggested to get married as soon as possible. "Just not this," she answered, suddenly realizing all the absurdity of any kind of escape in the world – she couldn't escape from herself, from her dreams, from the voice of her husband in the sinister silence of daybreak.

"Finally, I'll be closer to Radusya's and Marko's graves there," she said while saying good-bye to her brother and sisters, quite clearly aware that she is seeing them for the last time. "You've always striven to pretend as though you've wanted this yourself," the eldest sister wiped her eye with her finger.

They returned in some Russian military vehicles; my father didn't like the driver with braids on his shoulder boards, but he just tensely remained silent. The driver was an Odesan and the object of his inner hesitation was how to take advantage of the presence in the cab of a dame, the bitch had run off with the Fritzes, and maybe lay down underneath them, what am I's to do, too bad, she's already not that young and some grownup guy is staring at me with the eye of a raven, okay, nuts to you, go on living, I won't touch ya, "gimme your watch, gimme it!" He snatched with a scream to scare her, so as to take advantage of the situation.

This return of theirs was similar to an unconditional surrender, those same landscapes were rising in the opposite direction, the amount of ruins considerably increased, the transport trains were stuffed with drunken soldiers and trophy suitcases, this was reminiscent of the worst possible dreams: commandants' offices, train stations, lice, lines for permits – and a catastrophic decrease of days and shrinking together of Europe. Late autumn some day or other they knocked at the door, and this is how this absurd escape from Egypt ended, a journey to the future and back. The lock of her daughter's hair, the ring, and her cigarette case remained intact – what else could she want?

And what more should I want, one of the immediate consequences of this return?

10
Thriller

Beyond a doubt, my father was different from me.

In September of 1959 every evening he would walk to meet mother, who was taking evening accounting courses. He was twenty-nine, and mother was nineteen, and he called her *babe*. They had already lived together for more than two years (a somewhat strange combination of experience and youth), and *babe* finally got pregnant. All September she would go to her evening accounting classes, and *daddy* would go to get her closer to eleven, so as to accompany her home safe and sound. In those years (as in all the further ones), the nighttime city was poorly lit; unruly hooligans would wreck the lamppost lights all the time. The central part of the city consisted of one-storey homes and small stone buildings, mostly from the Austrian period. At night it was a dark labyrinth of reflections with nearly lunar landscapes. One of those nights in time the monument to Stalin near the railroad station square was obliterated without a trace – by morning just a hill remained; shortly after that it lovingly was turned into a flowerbed. Dangers lay in wait at every step, especially for young women. That's at least what my father imagined.

My father was far from being a cool dude. The only reason he would have a jackknife in his pocket was that every free moment in the forest he loved to practise tossing that knife and most often ended up throwing it where he aimed it (stumps of birch and pine trees, the silent dripping of sap). But that evening he didn't have a knife, about which only you and I know for the time being.

Somewhere between the synagogue (the club of the Medical Institute) and the then theatre (the popular play *Guelder Rose Meadow* had ended a half hour earlier, and everyone had gone home), three guys stopped him. They crawled out from somewhere in the darkness, as though out of a lunar crater. I suppose this could be similar to the appearance of the vampires in the famous Michael Jackson video – *two dudes with butch haircuts and a slut with an open bottle in her hand.* "You!" One of them addressed my father. "You got smokes?"

This was the time of the next migration – from the second half of the 1950s they were actively expanding the suburbs, the small apartment buildings were being populated by all manner of people arriving, for whom, accordingly, newer and newer plants and factories were built, along with places for cultural events and relaxation, and the military branch – and the amount of Russian language heard in the city noticeably increased over any other. In connection with the renewal and reshaping of the face of reality, the city authorities were deliberating to what to change the name of the city. Prykarpatsk and Komsomolsk-Prykarpatsky were suggested.

"Where's that fucking knife?" My father thought, checking his pockets. "Have a smoke," he gave them an open pack of "Pryma." "You, I'll take two," the first of them said and took six or seven. "If you need them, take them," my father answered to that, convinced he had left the knife at home, in the pocket of his forest work coat. They laughed a while, sharing the smokes among themselves. "Yous is lucky you had some," the other one said, and they started to snicker again, and the slut started laughing idiotically. At this point they could have parted ways – they were mercifully letting him go. But he asked – in the same even voice as his father had uttered his "Like hell they'll get me" – however, he permitted himself to ask: "And what if I didn't have any?" They stopped grinning and turned their faces towards him. "Yous'll see now," the second one drawled out.

After these words of his it's worthwhile to somewhat slow down the filming (it was just in those times that this device was entering into filmmaking vogue). So, we see a part of my father – the mentally astral one – that separates itself from him and begins to observe the irreproachably automatic actions of the body from outside himself. His body manages to fend off the enemy's first blow of and immediately lets loose an uppercut with his left hand (it was the era of boxing, there weren't yet any karate enthusiasts with their stupid cat-like yells) and then after that – a right hook. That was enough for the *dudes* to fly off in various directions. The *slut* began to shriek and raised her bottle, from which something poured out, against the blow. My father's body managed to fend it off one more time, and the bottle flew several metres and reverberating rolled along the sidewalk, without breaking for some reason. Father's body with sufficient ease shoved the slut to the side, where she stumbled and sat down next to her friend, who was lying on the ground. The other in the meantime had already picked himself up, crazily shaking his head. It was left for my father's body to run, which is what he did. He crossed Mickiewicz Square (the poet turned-green on a pedestal evidently was not there), and then he ran past the former Bristol Hotel, along the corridors of which the spirit of the great composer Denys Sichynsky used to wander, and just at Halytska Street understood that no one was pursuing him, after which the mentally-astral part of him returned into his body.

"Why are you shaking all over?" Mother asked him when he took her by the hand at the exit from the accounting school. "It's not the merry month of May," he answered with an adage he had once heard in the army.

And in truth, it was September just then, and for me, apparently, it wasn't too bad lying there, inside, waiting for everything in the world.

11
Threnos

While we are alive, there is no death, that kind-hearted guy Epicurus once affirmed. Just as it arrives, we already are gone. We miss Death by its going in the opposite direction – we could have continued to develop Epicurus' joke. We slip out from under Death's nose. Which, in fact, it does not have.

But, there is one overly weighty "but." That "but" does not let us take pleasure as much as we'd like from the wittiest discovery of the old Hedonist. The "but" lies in the fact that we are not alone. The "but" lies in the fact that death comes not to us, but to those next to us.

Even after his death my father remained himself – the same unassuming man, imbued with simplicity and modesty, with a reluctance to mention anything about himself, to trouble others, to cause anyone problems or to ask about something. Not a single time did he appear in the house at night, nor did he shine from the threshold or from the window as a flash of light, as some other corpses have done, especially over the course of the first three to nine days, when ties with the recently departed loved ones are still overly painful and they want to be near you, in those same rooms, near those same objects (a pack of "Pryma" cigarettes, a desk lamp, two decks of cards). He didn't even speak up – either at midnight or before dawn. He didn't hint at a single mystery, he didn't leave any doors open, he didn't call to meet at the terrace of Elsinore Castle.[18]

(My grandfather is another matter. Having lost over the course of less than a year his daughter and her husband, his wife became indifferent to God and changed her confession to a *confirmed* atheist. I already wrote that in those years she smoked a lot and – I didn't write about this before – to spite everyone she stopped going to church. But this *confirmed* person, my grannie, to her very death at every opportunity tried to convince those chatting with her that sometime at the end of the 1940s, in the winter, just before dawn, Marko had come to visit her. "It was as if he were talking from somewhere on our veranda, I was already awake, because I had to run off to work really early, when suddenly I heard his voice: "I'm here, I'm with you." Then just a shadow on the drapes – and that's the way she related it, that atheist. Grandfather came to see her at very opportune times – those were the most hellish days for her: horrible poverty, a life eating meagerly (everything she made went to her son's studies in the technikum),[19] loneliness, aging – and where has the little girl disappeared, who from that veranda had watched Archduke Franz Ferdinand in a cabriolet – add to that cold, darkness, winter, boring work with statistics of tuberculosis illness and cutting and sewing at night as an additional possibility for survival, along with that periodic summons to the KGB with unequivocal reports of intentions. This was extremely necessary for her – this otherworldly visit, this expressive voice of a faithful soldier, these words that left no doubts that "I am here, I am with you.")

My father appeared to me from time to time just in dreams – in the distant perspective of some other plot, just as unobtrusive, and from a distance: he turned around and went off somewhere, barely waving his hand, like saying he wasn't going to get in the way, keep on living. I recognize this in him, I know this well.

In childhood it seems I was overly attached to him – he was a grand teller of stories (over the years – they were the very same ones, repeated), the author of a thousand unwritten novellas, a forest hero (he was a forester by profession, from which nearly automatically his frequent absence from home followed, as well as his constant inclination for alcohol). His stories concerned several animals that were saved, a nocturnal pursuit by winter wolves, something else – a shooting, chases on horseback, campfires. (I remember, the devil take it, I remember that later lost cleverness of narration, the mastery of intonation, the prominence of details, the minutely measured pauses and virtuoso speeding up – the entire captivated circle of people listened tensely, and women just devoured him with their eyes, so much because his manner of telling turned out to be eroticism.) In the 1930s he grew up on illustrated westerns, his memory even in the 1970s was chock-full of distant American echoes (Arizona Jack, he said, Alaska Jim, Alabama Joe, and Buffalo Bill).

I don't recall in general how many hours I stood near the window of that very same veranda, gazing out from behind the street corner for his return. A naive sense of my being in this world lay in this: waiting for this appearance to happen, the very recognizable wave of his hand that first rose from behind the corner, that trapper's western gait. Sometimes people carried him in, he fell on the bed with his clothes still on, I took off his shoes. This was my curse, these odours of vodka and leather, of belts, uniforms, this confused chattering (Arizona Jack, son, Arizona Jack and Sitting Bull, son, and three shots at the poachers). I wouldn't have lasted a minute in this world if he suddenly were gone.

He and I made a pact. Never and to no one did I divulge how much he had drunk, if, when it happened, I was a witness and a co-participant of his all-day wanderings. For this in nearly every pub he would buy me a glass of dry wine, always the same one – Rkatsiteli.[20] I didn't refuse, though even without this I never would have sold him out. On the road I got drunk, got sober and again got drunk, the old kindly buffet ladies recognized me, friends of my father (in those days I would count them to have been a hundred thousand) respectfully greeted me with a handshake, and father in the meantime deeper and deeper dove into his stories, some of them I had heard for the tenth time, we returned home under the cover of darkness and, no longer needed by anyone besides ourselves, sat for a long time on the veranda, enveloped by cigarette smoke and a less and less legible verbal wickerwork (carbine loaded, blood on the snow, three kilometres up the mountain, and I have a shot-gun, like hell they'll get me, what damn report, you all go to…).

But by the end of the seventies I no longer wanted to or could listen to this, I was interested not in Kirwood but in Kerouac, I distanced myself from my father by my obligation to change with the times. (In reality a human life is terribly long, in fact we live not one, but several lives, each time jumping out of our previous incarnation somewhere – and all this still happens here, on this earth, without passing through the cor-ridors of death, with the very same name, with the very same *registra-tion*, with the very same personal number.) Right then, in the moment of distancing myself from my father and in general from everything of my father's, I first underwent the abrupt invasion of the future. It reclaimed me, tore me out with my roots, I abandoned the entire past (the house, the veranda, westerns, vodka nightmares, horrific waiting) and began to live on my own. Maybe that was my first great emanci-pation – I lost one of my strongest dependencies. But maybe not com-pletely so: it was not so much emancipation as it was disillusionment. The forest hero and charismatic story teller was falling apart before my eyes, disappearing into the past. What was left was an uncontrollably aging man, forgetful and slow, prone to eternal repetition of one and the same tales (from overuse they withered, became effaced, faded, lost their previous springiness and reliability), he was left as a chronic player of patience and a recluse ("Red and Black," "Solitaire" – two times, "Portrait Gallery" – exactly the same, and again from the begin-ning: "Red and Black," "Solitaire," "Portrait Gallery").

Maybe this was my first great betrayal. Maybe my first great loss. Our betrayals are at the same time our losses, but without them we do not exist.

Since then another twenty years have passed (an awful lot, an entire classic novel!), while he was alive. Only the distance between us never decreased again. Then there were still many hours over the course of which I phoned the hospital while he was dying. Until they told me "yes, overnight." (Several spasms with guttural sobs in the bathroom, where I bathed him for the last time on Monday – a little shaving brush caught my eye, and that's it, that's "all," but it was *his* shaving brush!)

12
Intermedia

"Young man, think faster, I have six more corpses today," said the lady from the undertakers. My father died at night on Good Friday, though quite inopportunely: a holiday, the biggest Christian holiday, was in full swing, and the working folks wanted to celebrate, and here these damn corpses, shit. "On Monday," I said. "What Monday, what Monday," the undertaker began to get irritated. "There's no priest who'll do a burial on Monday! It's such a big holiday, and you want to have a funeral. It's better for Tuesday! But by Tuesday he might begin to spoil. You see, what's the weather going to be? We had no spring and suddenly it's summer. How about tomorrow. Tomorrow's Saturday. Do it before the holidays. Have a funeral quick-quick – and you'll have peace of mind for Easter."

My buddies in the car were waiting for an answer. It was the first incredibly spring day at the end of an awful April. In the building there was a thick mixed scent of thawed water, squills, pine needles, candles, perfumes, and sweat. Under different circumstances I would have been gratified by such intensity (all the same I was gratified!). "I'll call home," I answered to her. "A couple of words."

Mother on the other end of the telephone line didn't get to the phone right away. "They're suggesting the funeral be tomorrow," I said. "They don't do funerals on Monday because it's a holiday. If not tomorrow, then it'd have to be Tuesday." The telephone line was antediluvian, the phone too. Black ebony.[21] Mother heard just crackling and separate words. I repeated myself three times. "… people will say … even not till … still try … you can't …," I heard. I understood and was thinking the exact same way.

"On Tuesday," I said, putting down the receiver. "If you can give us a van on Monday to take the body home from the hospital, then we'll have the funeral on Tuesday." "All right," the lady agreed. "They have a refrigerator at the hospital. He'll lie there properly. We also have one, but ours is stuffed. People are dying like crazy. Especially right before the holidays." I paid for the wreaths, ribbons, lettering on the ribbons, and left pieces of paper for the artist with the texts of the lettering (all the same I later found several mistakes). "You pay for the casket separately," the lady informed me, though without her saying it I knew. "The van to the hospital from us, Monday, ten a.m.," and she gave me a receipt. "Thank you," I said as I was leaving. "Happy holidays to you." "And to you too," she answered politely.

13
Intermedia-2

The coffin maker was sculpted out of some kind of poor quality dough – he kept swaying under his shirt, walking as though he were covered by undulating waves. He had a voice that was unexpectedly high-pitched. You find these types among argumentative provincial tenors or nasty clowns. "He's queer," Slavko whispered to me, concealing a mocking smile. "This kind or that?" The coffin maker showed two of his masterpieces of different lengths. "It's hard to say, judging by the eye," I shrugged my shoulders.

The caskets were high quality and apparently oak, singed with a soldering iron, and filled inside with fresh golden shavings. "How tall was he?" The coffin maker was impatient. "Shorter than me," I mentioned. "More or less like him," I nodded my head at another Slavko. "Like you. Nearly exactly," the first Slavko assured the coffin maker. "Like this?" The coffin maker immediately focused and with a flexibility unexpected for him lay down right in one of the caskets, it was just the right size. "Will you take this one?" Then he winked: "I'm allowed, it's my job. *What's the last name?*"

He scribbled the name on the coffin with a chemical pencil. I counted out twenty-seven new bills and gave them to him. He drove his axe into a wooden column and licked his finger. "Keeps *in mind*," he said, counting out the bills again, "it's *separate* for trimming and lace." I added the amount he wanted. "In order," he shoved the entire sum into the back pocket of his pants covered in sawdust. "When are you getting the *corpse*?" "Monday, ten a.m.," one of us said. "Okay, evrythin'll be snappy," he shifted his stomach and chest. "Where could I have seen you?" He fixed his eyes on me. "On television," I waved him away.

14
Mystery

It was, as I already wrote, Good Friday, a day when everything suddenly awakened and began to buzz after a month and a half of cold and snow with rain. The hospital was located nearly outside the city, on hills, the Medical Examiners Department was a bit farther out, at the edge of the hospital grounds, beyond it was just the wide-open world: the vertiginous perspective of the fields, the scent of the soil, of the first grass, a deep blue forest near a mountain, and finally the *promises of the Carpathians*, as Joseph Roth would have written, on the horizon. We waited for the end of the autopsy and received the medical certificate. On the basis of that certificate you'd receive a death certificate. On the basis of the death certificate – the right to hold a funeral. On the basis of this right – the right to our, putting it mildly, *rotation*.

The doctor had an unequivocal weakness for philosophizing. He stepped out to me on the porch already after everything had been done and, similar in appearance to one of Chekhov's doctors, true, without a pince nez, made a generalization: "You know, in such instances we are left with a tiny ray of relief – it's good that he ended his suffering. Who are you to him? His son?" For some reason I started to talk about an injection, that they needed to do an injection so the *body* would last longer, because it was not clear when we would be able to have the funeral, the holiday, etc., he interrupted me: "Did you give money to the guys?" I affirmed that. "Then no problem, he'll get the injection. Do you, pardon me for asking, believe in God?" But I didn't manage to answer, because he had just finished smoking and slapped me on my back, he moved off to do the next autopsy: they're dying like flies, sharp fluctuations in weather, the heart's blood vessels don't tolerate it.

The day unfolded like a succession of addresses and *stations*: the ZAGS (Bureau of Vital Statistics) office, the ceremonial plant, the *house of sorrow*, social insurance services, the church chancery, the post office. The wind warmed up incredibly quickly; in the afternoon everyone took their things off under the sun. They took off their outer layers of clothing, women instantly managed to jump into short skirts, Sheptytsky Square turned into a total parking lot and was jammed with cars. Ihor looked for half an hour for somewhere to squeeze into, it was good that the parking guard imbeciles turned out to be acquaintances, the centre of the city was just vibrating (buying things, trading, selling, sausages, hams, Paska Easter breads, eggs, sour cream, baskets, sacks, bags, kerchiefs, candles, icons, holy pictures, religious medallions – crosses), a several-hundred-metre-long line stretched to the cathedral for confession with communion; it was a true *conveyor of conscience* for you ("listen, how can they prostrate themselves on their knees in such short skirts?") . . .

But they normally stepped out onto the square after it all and, calmed down, and appropriately whispered to themselves: "… at the right hand of Your glory, for the sake of the prayers of Your Immaculate Mother and all the Saints."[22] And just then *the sun darkened, and for three hours there was darkness over the earth*. At three o'clock after noon (we had just been sitting in the reception office of social services, *Jesus began to call out in a strong voice: "Father, into thy hands I commend my spirit!" Then he bent over his head and died. At that moment the earth began to shake, cliffs fell, graves opened, and many corpses arose. And the centurion and those who had guarded Jesus with him, upon seeing the earthquake and what had happened, became terribly frightened and said: "Truly this was the Son of God!"*

15
Lamentation

That truly happened, I said to myself, it had to have happened once.

On Monday we brought the *body* home and put it on a table. (A *body*, just like that, a body, the entire time I caught myself for some reason saying and thinking "the *body*," while my mother continued to call it by his name.) Tens of people came over, entire layers of years, biographical offshoots, epochs, masks, roles. The forties, fifties, sixties, seventies, eighties. Those from the nineties were in the minority. Neighbours tried to convince us not to allow That One to see him, because she has the habit of stealing something (shoelaces, pins, handkerchiefs) from the deceased and later hiding them on living people, so as to cast spells. We didn't let her approach.

Death brings solidarity to those, who are left to live. The contemplation of death temporarily makes them close. Life soon after will cause everyone to argue with everyone else. But for the time being all for one, it's true that death cleanses you of the unessential.

"Let's put things there for him," mother said, "let's put his eyeglasses, playing cards, and a pack of cigarettes in there. And especially Rada's hair. They were brother and sister after all." "As you wish," I answered, "all this, in truth, is a kind of paganism, but as you wish." "In Eastern Ukraine," someone else intruded on the conversation, "they even put in a bottle of vodka. Everything the deceased loved in his life." "Vodka?" Mother was surprised. "That's already too much!" "But you're already putting in cigarettes," I wanted to remind her, and resigned myself: it's not clear how it will be with me eventually.

Vodka, vodka, everybody will get a double shot, everybody'll get seven each, shit, again the glasses are plastic, not a double-shot for me, but a triple, and mineral water for me as a chaser, two beers, any kind of juice, and coffee, and pizza, and pizza-shmeetza, and piss, kuokh-kuokh-kuokh and a smile for me, and all this outside, let your mopstick of a waitress carry all this outside, m-my, fuck, it's as though everything till now is all in formalin, a ball stuck in my throat. (My buddies helped bring the body from the hospital, carried it into the apartment, and requested they be granted their freedom. They felt considerably better in freedom, I was envious.) *Everybody do what you want, but I – If I don't drink, I'll croak. – Pour me another, why are you waiting – Why do we come into this world? – That's how I said it: horrors – I felt sick, then I sat down – They paint them up there in the corpse room – A normal concept – What's with your hands, old man? – Then pour, if nothing – Not repenting for the deceased – Until he's buried, you can't – Exactly, he's telling the truth – Then for Yurko: so that he survives this night – So that we all survive – There's nothing to carry there – Go take another one – They have that here for an extra charge – Better from a store – Then not one, but two – The worst there is the staircase – It's better not to die in these apartment buildings – Then they won't carry you out – O, I remembered an anecdote – yadda-yadda-yadda – What, you said it like that? – Good, I'll take another bottle if you ask those lit-tle – Christ is Risen, girls – And he did that right – uekh-uekh-uekh – Friends, I'm about to read a poem – This old guy's what, a poet? Pyotrova and Panova died – The angel of death is in the air – Don't love yourself, make a casket – And that should be a poem? – This is a poem! And you? Are you a sort of poet, buddy? And why are you so wet already? – I didn't understand – Go to hell you fucking cunt – What's she doing in the bushes – I'm taking off I know how to – I have two more double shots – And good-bye! – And it's dark like in a forest, and it's dousing Monday . . .*[23]

All this in its own way has been balanced out, because at the very same time another rite was taking place over father's body (over the course of the first two holy days the deacon nearly lost his voice and was barely able to wheeze, but on the other hand the priest was impec-cable): *Christ is risen from the dead! By death he has trampled death; and to those in the tombs he granted life. Christ is risen from the dead! By death he has trampled death; and to those in the tombs he granted life.*[24] And again, and one more time, and many-many times the same from the beginning.

16
Depression

Around the eve of your fortieth year of existence, as though coming into your house, death entered your life. You knew about it before, but so what? It was too far away and was allotted to everyone other than you. This was something that would happen only beyond the boundary of your world. But it appears, expands here around you, right around you, and now you begin to see clearly: from now on there will be more of her. Life has turned towards sunset, the sun is setting in the bays of silence – and there is not a day without her. Take a look at the dead: they are still here, in candles and flowers, and in truth they already are floating in their boats untied from the landings, they sway in their tunnels, weightless and enchanted. And it's fruitless to wait for their return, and no one is waiting.

It happened: you also suddenly have become conscious of your suspension between *plus and minus infinity*, immediately after many others, immediately everyone, who knew about death and lived with it inside. You joined the majority, became one of those to whom it suddenly sank in that this truly is a horror ("I know, there will be a bottom of a well there, a dark room without a tiny ray of light," a certain Polish agnostic jotted in his notebook). You physiologically, with all your being, sensed this horror of linear time (there is only one stream, one single direction of movement, and nothing returns, and never will you step into that same Danube, and you'll never stop a single moment, and youth will not return, and we have no choice). Here, finally the reason: we have no choice. Here it is, horror.

(You in a feminine way think about physical aging, you register every change tied to your fingernails, skin, hair, lashes, the weariness of your eyes and cheeks, the breakdown of your muscles, the unpardonable whimsicality of your penis, the arrhythmic leaps of your heart. In a feminine way you think about women, about their stares. At one time every step of yours was enveloped by the energy of those stares. Right away several female generations were looking at you – with expectancy, with testing, with a call, with a hint, with anticipation. Those caught stares are fewer now. In addition they've seemingly been covered with something sticky and depraved – those are the wrong and not the same kind of stares, sorry. It's you who've changed, crocodile.)

It's as though I prepared myself for this. I've read so much of everything, that it would be appropriate to burn all those books, and I've seen even more, I've gathered so many impressions, seconds, flashes, I've taught myself coldness and calm, I knew about the vanity of vanities. But why then does something press on me – from without? from within? And there are plenty of those phantoms all around my house, some kind of infinite rustling, howling, growling, they don't love me, scamps, they're just waiting to push me down, for the entire mob to pounce, to tear me to shreds, no one loves me. It was once upon a time, long ago, that everyone loved me.

And so you live – all from fear and sorrow, from epitaphs, from ruined cemeteries, from your central-European heritage, from alcohol and bravado, from a heavy, confused baroque, from black humour, from the grass of oblivion, from Yorick, from Calderón ("And what is a dream? Is not our entire life a dream?" – shouts in unison a certain ridiculous person, Dostoevsky). And is God a Worm to us?!

Our life, this miserable shade of the here and now, compressed beyond belief by two horrifying and inclined to growth massifs called the past and the future. These are the thicknesses that we are unable to imagine. This is eternity *before us* and eternity *after us*, this is a world *without us*. Undoubtedly, the emptiness after our disappearance is horrifying. But how is the emptiness before our appearance better, the hundreds of thousands of years of infusion in silence and darkness, in the cold laboratories of being? I don't know a greater loneliness than the loneliness of each of us, a greater emptiness than the emptiness that mocks us.

So what is the past, what is the future to me? I am abandoned to my own devices, I have come and will go. *I was a passer-by among you on the exalted street.*

But something remains. Something is passed on. I'm not talking about genes. Once in this world, not very far from me (and at times intolerably close from me), my father used to live. Now he is no longer here, but something is there all the same: an intonation, a gesture, the word order in a sentence, a pause, the timbre of his voice, a cough. This is me, him, this is everyone who came before and will come after us. Here I look out from a hillock onto the forest – and I forget about everything, I grow still, silent. And suddenly: isn't this *him* looking at the forest, isn't this *his* gaze?...

17
The Choir

A stare, a sweep of the hand, an old cracked postcard, the scent of ruins, a stroll with loved ones, a white dog on a white snow, the shadow of a bird on the road – signs are given to us. We are sustained in our emptiness, in our loneliness. Everything isn't so tragic, the angels love us.

Fortunately I live in a part of the world where the past is awfully important. Some call this *rootedness*, and others – *obsession*. I don't know myself what to call this: simply in this part of the world there are too many ruins, too many skeletons under your feet. Fortunately, I can't free myself from this. It's hard for me to imagine a sterile person – a clean sheet of paper, not sullied by anything, without a single bloody spot, without a single spasm in your throat. I'm not worth anything without my memory, this is a land where I have all too much of everything (lines of poets, the wine of ruins, my first love, my last love, a hundred cities where I remained forever, in my memory my father, the veranda, two decks of cards), too much of everything, without which there is not and would not be me. Such a future is hideous to me, in which none of this would be.

The past century quite consistently taught me to be wary of lofty and overly accountable words. It turned out to be an ideal teacher of a lack of faith and – inevitably – unbelief that went after a lack of faith. In speaking about the future, I will acquiesce to a word less doubtful than the word "faith." Than even "love." The correlate of the future in us is hope, the same way as memory is present in us a correlate of the past.

The human formula is memory plus hope. However, why have addition here, and multiplication, what other arithmetic? These simply are two entities with which we cover ourselves in emptiness. But finally, we do not cover ourselves – in reality we tear off of ourselves all kinds of shells, we cross over boundaries. Openness is the only thing that is left for us to find at least some understanding with others, with everything that is around us and inside us. An openness to life, an openness to death, an openness to the past, and an openness to the future.

My memory allows me to do everything that I desire. My hope knows no bounds. I mix up times, turn the pages of decades, I displace expanses, and populate the planes of the intersection with life.

So, let there be summer, we are travelling along the damp foothill plane somewhere in the Danube Basin, here right near the centre – of Europe and each of us, a human "I" lies in the central-eastern part of the body, we buy countless bottles of cheap but tasty wine, red and white, an old German for the Hutsuls is doing the paintings for a church in a village not far from the mountain pass, this is his last order, poor Karl – the apostles Petro (Peter) and Yakiv (Jacob) are finally turning out well for him, gates open one after another, bridges are lowered, on the other side of the Danube the world seems newer and bigger, Chicago is real to you, there are hillsides of grapes, and a path leads to a castle, this is a track and a conjecture, this is a Templar's rose garden, frozen sand in hourglasses, the balls of a mechanical billiard table frozen in pockets, planes stopped in mid-air over a train, a stopped train, an engraver standing still over a silver signet ring, the circling of birds over Poprad and Prater, we drink from the bottles and barely keep from dancing on the ruins. We summon the rain, but that's not enough for us – we summon the sun, a boy's voice breaks and there will be so much more of everything – waiting for dirty diesel local trains at tiny stations, swimming in greenish rivers, making love under thousand-year-old yew trees, while the scowling blond-haired hero is walking from the field, having made his decisive goal, while my father and I are walking through the meadow overflowing with sunlight, I'm twenty, he's forty-two, and frogs are jumping from right under our feet into small roadside lakes, while my father and I go through Prague, Budapest, Krakow, Lviv, we take city after city – and we stop in everywhere for homemade wine, because we loved to drink together, in this way objects become symbols, and symbols – objects, and for the last time I wipe his shoulders with rough bast, the water in the bathtub is a little too hot, tomorrow will already be too late, he says, but maybe I just seemed to hear it.

Maybe we're too noisy by these ruined walls?

"The appearance of a rainbow!" the director commands, that is, *The Director*. We still have an awfully long time to live – this apparently is the universe, these distances can't even be compiled in your head. I stop the film and I stop time: the here and now.

But this is not just the here and now. This is also the past, this is a time, when there was no death, this is the lightness of inexperience and the mixing of wine. This is also the future, from which I, different, look at all this. This is the fullness of times – three in one, as they say now. This is the space of the coexistence of time and eternity. And there, where we succeed in this, where we reach that fullness at least by a half-note, we, perhaps, finally become ourselves.

(*By the way, in reality everything wasn't quite like that. As the notes in the report to our dean attested, we got completely soaked by the rain, our shirts stuck to our backs, our legs were ready to fall off from the thirty-kilometre march, in addition we mixed up the red and white wine really badly, in the wrong proportions and in the wrong consistency. As a result of that, our heads ached, and we all, in fact, argued with each other – going one by one into the forest, walking along the roadside, and while returning to the city by train, we remained silent and avoided looking at each other in the eye.*)

If that matters.

18
A Quotation

There remains only the beginning of someone else's poem. Something needs to be done with it – somehow add to it.

To free the future from the past?
To free the past from the future?

Something remains to be written either after these lines, or before them:

To free us from us?
To free me from me?
To free the human from his skeleton?

September 1998–January 2000
Expanded version 2005

Culturological and Political Essays

Erz-Herz-Perz

TRANSLATED BY MARK ANDRYCZYK

1

The family stories that are the least believable are the ones we remember the best.

As a twelve-year-old girl, my grandmother Irena Skochdopol saw Archduke Franz Ferdinand riding in an open car. Led by an escort of cavaliers and by the captivated stares of countless inhabitants of Stanislaviv, lined up on both sides of Romanovsky Street (Romanowski-gasse), the heir to the Austro-Hungarian throne, together with his wife and a few vice-heirs in the back seat of his, let's say, Lorraine-Dietrich, set off towards the train station, from which he was to take a nighttime express train to Chernivtsi. But why to Chernivtsi? Leisurely glancing today at a tattered map of the Empire's railway lines it becomes quite clear that going through Chernivtsi was not the best route. I'll venture to guess: the Archduke and his family took a different route – past the impressive, oil-filled tracts and the hydrogen sulfide mineral springs, passing the rain-soaked and mushroom-scented thickets of the Black Forest, towards Morshyn, Stryi, and Hrebeniv, and then directly south so that, at the onset of dawn, they could immerse themselves into the ancient and night-splashed shimmer of the Gorgans (the Beskyds?), arriving the next morning at the territory of the Alföld, the Great Hungarian Plain where Óbuda, Buda and Pest, and an abyss of wineries, already awaited him, with their fiery foods and moving music. And life went on. The last stop was Sarajevo.

But let us return to the twelve-year-old girl, raised by the Basilian Order of Nuns, the daughter of a Ruthenianized Sudeten German half-Czech (yes, such a possibility did exist), who loved to go to the

Fotoplastikon,[1] to cross-stitch and to read Camille Flammarion's popular astronomy guide. Her impressions from seeing the Archduke, or, as
it is in its Ukrainian version – the Archprince – from the window of her
father's veranda, were drawn simply in a few short strokes.

Late afternoon July, 5 p.m., a recent rain settling the surrounding dust
and refreshing the plants and rocks. Both sides of the sidewalk are filled
with people greeting representatives of the dynasty with the waving of
handkerchief-flags. Brilliantly polished (just like a fireman's) helmets
of the cavalry and equally shiny, well-fed, and well-trained horses.
The weak (why weak?) hand of Ferdinand dangles over the door, it
exists on its own, separate from his body, occasionally jerking to wave
in response. Mrs Archprincess in her "Jugendstil" Viennese hat with
its embellishments, her face hidden under a veil, with a smile, which
all present determined to be a motherly one. It's strange – grandma,
who was just a child then, didn't recall anything in particular about
Ferdinand's children. Occasionally, loosely describing the sailor's out-
fit worn by one of them, but that, I think, was just the layering of that
Fotoplastikon or, later – the cinematograph . . .

I paint in the rest myself. Most important for my project are – a gentle
breeze, an evening wind, the flight of quiet angels, giving everything
a fleeting, almost tattered look, everything waves and shakes – plum-
age on dragoons, feathers on the gendarmes, hetmans' banners, tails
and manes, forelocks on the uncovered heads of Christians and long
curls on Jews, traditional Ukrainian embroidered cloths and even one
blue and yellow ribbon,[2] and an innumerable amount of other ribbons
and, as has already been described, flags and handkerchiefs. Everyone
is allowed to take part in the festivities – and even Mrs Kapitanova, the
crazy hygienist, well known in the city, who would wash her clothes
publicly, everywhere and all the time and even old man Oliynyk, who
fixed umbrellas and drank beer for a hundred years in a row, and even
the gymnasium professor Dutka, who knew nineteen languages – all
of them are present in this idyllic evening scene, under the invisible
wings of the empire. And no anarchist, no assassination attempt or self-
sacrificing bombing, no shootings, no secret group or illegal clan – this
world order seems to be the only possible, certain and stable one, the
empire seems to be immortal, while the terrorist Sichynsky[3] will already
have been living somewhere in America for a few years – where all the
world's terrorists and criminals are supposed to live.

Photographs from that time, it seems, do not provide evidence that
either denies or confirms the picture I have painted. This episode of

Ferdinand's visit and subsequent departure has remained but an episode –
with no lesson learned and without even any anecdotal effect. All that
remains is a mood, a fleeting notion, an impression, an aftertaste – but
these things are so subjective that it's difficult to glean any useful, philosophical generalization from it.

Let's move on to things that are more objective.

2

The attitude of Galician Ukrainians towards the old Danube monarchy
was neither hostile nor idealistic but rather ironic. This irony begins at
the level of the emperor's portraits hanging in many Ukrainian living
rooms (framed by traditional Ukrainian embroidered cloths, of course,
like the portrait of Shevchenko next to it), and ends with completely
senseless, and thus harmless Russophilism.

Of all the elements of an inevitable future explosion, with which the
Austro-Hungarian Empire was filled because of its bickering patchwork character, the Ukrainian element was the least explosive. This
does not mean that it was not explosive at all – the example of the
already-mentioned student Sichynsky, who rather resolutely, and
without any particular Raskolnikov-like torment, killed Count Potocki, the Governor of Galicia, thus turning the latter's nine children
into orphans, attests to the fact that "we're no worse than they are."
Nonetheless, this criminal episode had more of an anti-Polish character than an anti-Austrian one (yet another example of the eternal and
mutually exhausting Ukrainian-Polish "an eye for an eye, a tooth for
a tooth").

For me, the apologia of "deceased Austria" ("mommy Austria," as
those same Galicians would joke) begins with the belief that it is thanks
to her that the Ukrainian component of the boundless linguistic-national
diversity of the world has been preserved. This may have happened
against her will, but we would not be here today if it were not for her.
Humankind would be one culture, one mentality, and one language
poorer. And that fact itself, I believe, makes that most enlightened one,
Emperor Franz Joseph I, worthy of a Nobel Prize in the Noosphere, if
such a prize were given posthumously or if it were given at all.

Second, inside this preserved language, thanks to this most frivolous
of empires, a dialect has been preserved that has as one of its characteristics an exquisite collection of tasty, clear Germanisms beginning with
"fana," "fertyk," "fryshtyk," and "farfotsli" and ending with the almost

sacral "shliak by ioho trafyv" (may lightning strike him). And what would I, a Ukrainian writer, do without these Germanisms?

Third, it is thanks to her, this non-existent grandma, that many things that could not be pacified and united were indeed pacified and united. Because of its patchwork and mixed nature, because of its belonging, both biological and historical, to everything in the world, it was a real "circus of anomalies" and a travelling collection of the exotic and the abnormal. She was forced to choose liberty and pluralism for herself, providing shelter for practically everyone – from Hassids to Old Believers, from mysterious Karaites to absolutely ordinary Maramureş Gypsies – she was perhaps the first to ban persecution based on race, nationality, or religion.

Fourth, she preserved architecture for us – different and various, she preserved different cities, she preserved the right of these cities to continue to exist, resulting in them stubbornly not wanting to be ruined regardless of all the situations that were conducive for ruining and because of this my Stanislaviv does indeed (praise be to God!) look different than Dnipropetrovsk, Kryvyi Rih, or Zaporizhzhia.

Fifth and finally, she opened up new geographic possibilities for us and taught us to look West with love for its tender twilight. Just think about it – there was a time when my city belonged not to the same state entity that included Tambov or Tashkent, but to the one that included Venice and Vienna! Tuscany and Lombardy belonged within the same border as Galicia and Transylvania. At the beginning of the century, I would not have required a visa in order to meet up with Rilke, or, let's say, Gustav Klimt; to get off a train in Cracow, Prague, Salzburg, or Trieste, I would only need a corresponding train ticket. I ask anyone who doubts this to look at that map of the imperial-royal railway system that I already mentioned.

In my view, these are the five main points in defence of our Austro-Hungarian history. Actually, there could be many more such points and they could be quite different – I would be more than happy if they were to supplement me or correct me. Or even contradict me.

3

An old Galician anecdote (anecdotes in the way that Oleksandr Irvanets uses Pushkin's "anecdotes of bygone days") tells the following story. A group of recruits from Galicia was brought in to supplement the Austrian army. The first military lessons consisted of learning the names and titles of the higher command. A toothy corporal made it clear to the Ruthenian recruits that the commander of their regiment was the Arch-prince knight Toskansky, in German "erzherzog ritter von Toscana." Then, he made a very large young man from the environs of Zhab'ie or Prokurava, who was as big as a bear, repeat this. Without batting an eye, the young man said "Erz-herz-perz, ripa z motuzkamy!"

I don't want to go on about the fact that, in the Hutsul dialect, the word "ripa" mentioned above, means not turnip, as is the case in liter-ary Ukrainian language, but something completely different – it means potato. Moreover, I will not analyse how much better the Austrian army was prepared for battle after that lesson taught by the corporal. But I do want to generalize at least a bit: within that "erz-herz-perz," as in a magic incantation, so many things are concentrated: here we have the aforementioned irony, and the characteristic Ukrainian village nature, a rustic cleverness applied to the strange and to strange languages, and a playful naughtiness, a certain "Švejking."[4] But for me this also serves as a diagnosis. In it is our accumulated backwardness, a fatal tiptoeing at the doorway of Europe with an inability to move forward through it, a prophesy that contains all caricature and parody of everything we do in art, in politics, and in the economy. An all-encompassing "erz-herz-perz" that is everywhere.

This can be considered to be the result of a childhood stuck in time. Or old age dementia. Or a colonized past. "Ukraine still needs to settle its own cities," I wrote back in 1991, thinking then that this was going to happen very soon. Today, I look at the situation much more pessi-mistically, doubting that the children of my children will be living in Ukrainian cities.

4

Stanislaviv is near Tysmenytsia. Galicia's third largest city, following Lviv and Cracow, lies between the Gold and Black Bystrytsia rivers, like Babylon does in Mesopotamia. Its downtown and nearby streets are lined with two-storey buildings (for the most part), promenades, casinos, and shops with exotic goods, cafés with Colombian coffee, pastry shops with candied fruit and biscuits. Churches: Greek Catho-lic (cathedral), Roman Catholic ("Fara"), Armenian, Lutheran, a syna-gogue with four cupolas constructed in the Mauritanian style. Statues of Mary the Mother of God and of John the Baptist, erected in honour of the retreat of the Russians in 1742. A statue of Christ the Saviour in memory of the great plague of 1730. A bronze statue of Emperor Francis I. The city library that includes, among others, over eight thousand volumes of historical works alone. Hotels: "Union," "Central," "Europe," "Habsburg," "Imperial." Single-storey villas surrounded by flower gardens. The most popular street, Lindengassee, or Linden St – leads to the Empress Elizabeth city park.

I am referencing concrete facts. These details come from an early-twentieth-century small-railway travel guide. These are very brief yet very clear details. They contribute to the completeness of the picture.

Your basic city. Somewhere between "a city" and "a town." Joseph Roth's heroes visited cities like this in order to bed yet another maid on their way to New York.

It almost doesn't exist anymore today. It hangs onto that "almost," still demonstrating a suspicious trend towards restraint and endurance. That's why we still have those cracks in the fortification walls, those collapsed roofs, those trees growing in stairways, those stained glass fragments and marble tiles underfoot.

Our local apocalypse began not too long ago – in September of 1939, when abandoned to the winds, "upper-class" homes were settled by other people, the newly arrived from far away plains, where one-eyed giants with eight fingers live, where they drink vodka like water, even instead of water, where they eat raw meat, and dancing bears perform in churches . . .

The easiest thing to do was to just move in. To break into these secession-era villas, into the luxury of large constructivist buildings, into one-storey, eclectic single-family homes. The easiest thing to do was to just grab furniture, porcelain, walnut wardrobes with wrappers, toppers, *pantofle*, and slippers, shellac records, and vinyl records, clocks, undecipherable but dangerous books with impeccable book markers made of cigarette paper, oil paintings and small gypsum statues from haberdashery stores – in other words, all this culture, this whole collection of everyday stuff, which the newly arrived treated with an easygoing, proletarian disdain, disrespecting form, simply for what it is – but, for some reason, they expressed their disdain through possession.

But the newly arrived didn't consider that taking over dwellings also brings a certain responsibility to care for them. That these walls, doors, and mansard roofs require consistent and diligent care. That unfamiliar plants in gardens and on patios need to be looked after, that rare birds should not be shot with pneumatic weapons, and that philosophers and poets should not be shot with firearms either.

This complete, functional everyday irresponsibility led to the ruin of not only buildings. The city was being carted off to the East in whole echelons. I'm adding the fascist occupation here as well, which led to the complete "cleansing" of one of the city's most important ethnic components – the Judaic. Instead of refined and artistic, dreamingly-deep, melancholic, adherents of Hassidism, after the war, an innumerable amount of plain, Sovietized Jews – already Russian-speaking, already codified, already ashamed of and distancing themselves from their Jewishness.

Finally, I will add but one fact, the most "unpatriotic" one." The factor of the surrounding Ukrainian village, which came to these territories towards the end of the 1950s – inhabiting cramped, soulless, new buildings and successfully making them cultureless, preserving all the worst elements of village life and losing all the best. This newest wave of invasion, it seems, has only recently abated, when life in the city is becoming too expensive and hopeless. On the other hand, it is they, these village invaders, who triggered the advent of a completely different linguistic situation. I'm intentionally not saying here whether this is good or bad, although I should be saying that this is good. It's just that there are too many of the dead underfoot.

Because if that is how dwellings were dealt with, it is easy to imagine what took place with temples and cemeteries. Family grave plots, as well as anonymous mass burial sites, turned out to be equally useful for "erasing borders." Some old-timers still remember when, at the end of the 1940s, the embalmed Count Joseph Potocki was carried out from beneath the "Fara"[5] Church, in a cherry-red coat and a feather-adorned Hungarian cap embroidered in gold. That mummy, together with a huge pile of old church holdings was loaded onto Polutorka trucks and taken to an unknown location.

What has happened in the last fifty years is beyond comparison even to such major catastrophes as the "marmalade fire" of 1868, when, as a result of the negligence of a daydreaming housewife, who was cooking marmalade on a low flame in a courtyard at the beginning of Batory St, nearly the whole city burned down.

And it almost does not exist today. Yet it does still exist.

5

My Polish friend, an interesting young poet, sent me a pretty good art journal that includes his translation of my poem "Forgetting" from the cycle "July Notes of a Traveler." Having finished reading the translation, I understood why that particular poem was chosen. I provide it here, in its entirety, trusting that this won't be judged as petty self-love. Here it is:

> *It's as if a gate – is an entrance.*
> *There are cities that you cannot*
> *enter through a gate.*
> *There are cities that you cannot*
> *enter.*
> *And they bring a large key, and look for*
> *where to insert it, but*
> *there are no gates, the guards worn*
> *to dust. Seven winds luxuriate on squares and in halls.*
> *The city limits are open, the guards*
> *grow green and firm.*
> *"Zamarstyniv, Kulparkiv, Klepariv," –*
> *you list almost out loud,*
> *but you just can't recall the name*
> *of the tree*
> *to which she no longer goes ...*

In this Polish translation, everything is preserved except for the last line. Apparently, a purely intimate and very concrete erotic motif (because all I had in mind was that, as a young man, I really did walk up to a certain tree where I had a rendezvous with a certain girl), this personal motif was deemed to be no good for my translator, apropos, who comes from a family of former Lvivites, that is Lvivian Poles, who were resettled in Poland after World War II. And this is how the last stanza of this poem looks in his Polish translation:

> *"Zamarstyniv, Kulparkiv, Klepariv,"*
> *you list increasingly louder,*
> *but you just can't recall,*
> *the name of the tree*
> *from which (they) grow...*

That girl from my youth has just flown away. There is no mention of her. Something else, more weighty and difficult has taken her place instead: individual memory, more accurately non-memory, has transformed itself into historical memory, a historical memory that is insulted, if I may add, because for my Polish friend, Zamarstyniv, Kulparkiv, Klepariv (as well as, probably, Maiorivka or Levandivka) – are branches of Lviv's suburbs, which without doubt stem from a certain historical tree, that has the pleasant-sounding name "semper fidelis."

I am aware that this is in no way about any Polish territorial pretensions. Except, perhaps, a certain poetic territory. Therefore I am deeply grateful to my Polish friend – he once again identified poetry as a chance in this fragile world.

One truly can write about today's Lviv or Stanislaviv (and also about Stryi, Drohobyvh, or Buchach) as if about a pile of ruins, a kingdom of death, forgetting, and the all-triumphant Boor. But you can also write about other things: about life, about the daily battle against ruination, about making love by the crumbling walls and pockmarked frescos, about lively drinking parties and nighttime adventures in the gaps of old fortress alleys, about the resonance of ancient words that are nonetheless audible and discernable: "erz-herz-perz." And I am not to blame that such lively poems about Lviv or about Stanislaviv are being written today in the Ukrainian language.

Culture is indivisible – I am not the first and probably not the last to say this. At the beginning of the twentieth century, the extravagant leader of Young Poland, Przybyszewski, once got down on his knees before Vasyl Stefanyk in a certain Cracow café and kissed his foot. Let's leave outside the brackets of this episode the large amount of what had been drunk beforehand – it is present but not essential. Let's look at the gesture itself – artistic and human at the same time. That type of combination is quite rare.

Perhaps might it be precisely here, in this "buffer zone," in this ruined corridor between Western and Eastern Europe, where we will be able to do something similar more frequently?

1994

The City-Ship

TRANSLATED BY MARK ANDRYCZYK

It's unlikely that King Danylo Halytsky, the founder of Lviv, knew that the terrain that he had chosen for the strangest of all future cities of the European East had one very interesting geographic feature. I remember the all-encompassing and almost childlike fascination that overtook me the minute I found out about it. To me this feature seemed especially symbolic and not at all coincidental. The arrow launched from his royal bow in the middle of the thirteenth century landed right "in the bull's eye."

The essence of the aforementioned feature lies in the fact that through the city's territory, along its hills, which are almost entirely covered with cobblestones and fortification walls, runs the watershed between two basins of two seas – the Baltic and the Black. The peak of the watershed, invisible today, is located a few hundred metres from the main train station, or as they call it here in Lviv, from the *dvirets*. All rivers north of this point flow to the Baltic, while those south of it, to the Black Sea. The place of intersection of these two axes, which divide this unnamed space into East-West and North-South, naturally became the place of intersection of two trade routes, and, consequently, also the object of all sorts of invasions – spiritual, political, military, ritualistic, linguistic. The German name of the city – Lemberg – does not mean the same thing as the Latin Leopolis or the Sanskrit Singapore. This too marks its "watershed character" – the belonging to many cultures simultaneously while also not belonging completely to any of them – of the city, which a certain well-known novelist of the interwar years called "a city of erased borders." I, however, am attempting to avoid the rather simplistic temptation today to call it "a city of newly constructed borders."

Instead, let's use an entirely opposite metaphor – not a watershed (which divides) but something (I don't know yet, exactly what) that unites. For politicians, this could be an opportunity once again to discuss the Baltic–Black Sea concept. But I'm not a very good politician – more precisely, I'm not a politician at all. Thus, I'd like to think and talk about something altogether different. For example, about Lviv's municipal sewer system – the Poltva River: around three hundred years ago ships from Gdansk and Lübeck sailed upon it, and snake-like Atlantic eels were fished out of its waters by hand. And one hundred years later this river was buried underground. In this sense, Lviv is the exact opposite of Venice. The lack of water is felt so acutely here that the inhabitants of the oldest districts propagate a certain myth about Someone, Who could change wine into water. This sweltering drama reaches its culmination in August. The only sources of salvation then are the surrounding forests and parks with their ancient, truly regal, plant life, hidden lakes here and there, lilies and their secret healing springs – forests, lakes, lilies and springs, which, by the way, are disappearing.

This is the South breathing, increasingly hotter as it approaches. The architectural environment of Lviv is rather Latin, rather Roman, rather Baroque. In Soviet times, movies set in Paris or Rome were actually filmed in Lviv. If the setting was London or Stockholm, it was filmed in Riga or Tallinn.

Lviv is filled with the atmosphere of medieval culture – you just need to look for it. The winged lion of St Mark on the building of the Venice consul Bandinelli (on Rynok Square), like the Florentine courtyard or the exquisite emerald Dominican cupola don't seem at all exotic on the city's map. Beginning with the sixteenth century, its face was formed by various Italian exiles, fortune-hunters, wanderers, and adventurers, filled with the ideas of Renaissance humanism, epigones of flourishing Quattrocento, all those swashbuckling heroes such as Pietro di Barbona, Paolo Dominici Romanus, Ambrosio Prykhylny, or Callimachus Buonaccorsi.[1]

Byzantine-Greek accents are, to a great degree, fleshed out, or rather, balanced out, by Roman accents. And this doesn't just refer to the Byzantine traditions of Ukrainian churches. It refers to a particular Byzantine mentality, which may be the most crucial barricade blocking our integration into Europe, but may also be our most crucial defence against this integration. It is like the Cathedral of the Dormition with its Kornyakt Bell Tower – it can't just be rubbed, or crossed, out.

However, our journey South does not end there. I have not yet mentioned the Armenians, who re-immigrated to Lviv from Crimea, where militant Islam left them with increasingly less room for churches and shops. It is from them that the city acquires the roots of its Oriental foundation. Persian rugs made in Lviv were considered more beautiful than, well, actual Persian ones, not to mention fragrances, or various aromas – ginger, cardamom, saffron, pepper, musk, cinnamon; it was the Armenians who established the presence of spices in Lviv city life. But, nobody, it seems, has deciphered and read the gravestones of the old Armenian cemetery, while rumour has it that there are things stated there that are profoundly sagacious and needed by us. 1946, the year the Bolsheviks liquidated the Armenian-Catholic archeparchy, marks the end of the existence of the Armenian community in Lviv.

And Hebrews appeared in Lviv even earlier than the Armenians, at the end of the fourteenth century. They were not just clothing salesmen, tavern-keepers, and moneylenders, but, as Sebastian Fabian Klonowic branded them with great perturbation in his sixteenth-century Latin poetic lines:

The way rust eats at iron, and moths at clothing/The indolence of Jews destroys, ruins all . . .

In fact, there were learned Talmudic scholars and astrologers among them, as well as, I trust, the keepers of Chaldean wisdom, the possessors of secret knowledge. The last of them were destroyed by the Nazis in the 1940s and those who replaced them were plain, Soviet, de-ethnicized Jews. That Galician Jew, who no longer exists, gave birth to many extraordinary literary individuals, including Joseph Roth, the nostalgic essayist Józef Wittlin, and, without a doubt, Bruno Schulz – an unexpectedly rich fruit with a perversely sweet aftertaste.

And who else sailed on this ship?

Germans, or, as they were called here, "Schwabs," left their trace in the twisted names of Lviv's suburbs. What we refer to today as Lychakiv, actually comes from Luetzenhof, Zamarstyniv from Sommerstein, Klepariv from Klopper, Maiorivka from Majer, Kulparkiv from Goldberg, etc. And there was also the owner of a winery in Zamarstyniv with the striking last name Makolondra, and there was Josepha Kuhn, a Benadictine nun, author of the poetry collection *Lembergs schöne Umgebungen*, that is – "The Beautiful Suburbs of Lviv."

And who else ended up here, in these ship cabins and in hulls, on decks and masts?

Perhaps, it would be best simply to list them?

They include: Serbs, Dalmatians, Arnauts, Argonauts, Tatars, Turks, Arabs, Scots, Czechs, Moors, Basques, Scythians, Karaites, Khazars, Assyrians, Etruscans, Hittites, Goths, White and Black Croatians, Celts, Antes, Alans, Huns, Kurds, Ethiopians, Cyclopians, Agrippians, Laestrygonians, Androgyns, Aryans, Gypsies, Cynocephali, Elephantophagi, Africans, Mulattos and Mestizos, Little Russians, Muscophiles, and Masochists. The Franciscans, the Capuchins, the Barefoot Carmelites, and – of course, if I may – the Footwear Carmelites, the Bernardines, the Poor Clares, the Ursulines, the Sacramentarians, the Cecilians, The Dominicans, the Basilians, the Rastafarians, the Redemptorists, later the Jesuits, and even earlier, the Trinitarians, who were dedicated to buying out Christian captives from Eastern slavery. The Rosicrucians, the Studite Brethren, the Templars, the Old Believers, the Orthodox, and the Sinistradox.

I am convinced that all of them managed to somehow find themselves here. But I only mentioned some of them, and my list is by no means complete.

Because Lviv lies at the centre of the world. That Old World that was flat, that was held up by whales, or, in other versions, by a turtle, and its farthest suburb was India, onto the shores of which the waves of the Danube-Dunai, the Nile or, perhaps even, the Ocean splashed.

Even Lviv's plant life has preserved the incontestable characteristics of this "everything-ness." The Baltic pine and the Crimean cypress peacefully coexist in Lviv gardens, all of which could simply be termed botanical.

We, humans, are creatures that are inconsiderate and ungrateful, and always destined to lose something. We never truly value what we have, what we have been given from above.

One of my favourite books, Ivan Krypiakevych's *Istorychni prokhody po L'vovi* (Historical Strolls through Lviv), includes a very sad chapter about temples that no longer exist. Sometimes I ask myself: if this book had been written not in 1931, but today, how much longer and more horrible would that chapter be? I find Lviv to be incomplete without (I painfully miss) the Golden Rose Synagogue. I find it to be incomplete without the Tatar mosque and cemetery, once located somewhere near High Castle[2] – it's still there in the descriptions of collectors of impressions who visited in the seventeenth century. I find it to be incomplete because of many other things that once took place, including the annual Lviv carnivals, and the Sunday beggars' banquets, and the semi-fantastic zoo located in the Pohulianka neighbourhood.

Some of us try at least to recover them in a poetic line. But they, as a rule, don't allow it and slither away. Because Lviv really is a ghost ship.

The idealistic and painless mixing of cultures is but a myth. And I'm not sure that this myth isn't dangerous. Let us refer to a classic – this is what he wrote about such mixing: "If someone can't fall asleep at night in our city then let him enter the realm of the nighttime voices. The bells of the Catholic cathedral ring sharply and with conviction: it's two in the morning. And just over a minute later ... only then the softer, yet convincing voice of the Orthodox church makes itself be heard, also announcing that it is two in the morning. After a brief pause, one can hear the hoarse, distant sound of the clock on the mosque, but it rings 11 o'clock, some secretive Turkish time of day, in accordance with some distant, strange and chimerical countdown of time. The Hebrews don't have a clock on their tower, and God only knows whether their chronometers ring according to Sephardic time or Ashkenazi time."

This is Ivo Andric, and the nighttime city he is referring to is Sarajevo. And I won't say another word about it.

The stratification of cultures is not just the celebration of erased borders – it's also blood, dirt, ethnic cleansing, cannibalism, deportations. I probably misspoke and should have instead spoken about "the stratification of anti-cultures." Because this too is unavoidable in polyethnic communities.

When, in the middle of the eighteenth century, an ostentatious baroque church was built on St George's Hill, a major architectural entity was established that was now visible throughout the city. This, of course, irritated many Roman Catholics because the St George's Cathedral belongs to worshippers of the Eastern Rite. Payback came just under two hundred years later on Pryvokzalnyi Square, when the tall tower of the neo-Gothic Polish St Elżbieta Church, shot up like a rocket into the Lviv air, blocking St George's Cathedral from view from the train station. Since then, the panorama of St George's Hill has no longer been visible for people arriving to Lviv by train. Those collectors of impressions have now lost one more impression. This is another example of the aforementioned stratification. Of cultures or anti-cultures? What is there more of here – religious stubbornness, haughtiness, a clash in creativity, the desire to own? I don't know the answer, but I am sure that it is impossible to imagine the Lviv of today without that pseudo-gothic, kitschy "Elżbietka."

In the street battles over Lviv in 1918 the Poles defeated the Ukrainians because, to a large extent, it was their city – not in some kind of abstract-inhuman sense, but in the most concrete, personal sense – these were their doorways, courtyards, winding streets, they knew them like the back of their hands because it is there that they and their girlfriends had their first romantic encounters. The Ukrainians, supported only by the general-patriotic idea about the "princely glory of our Lviv," mostly came from the villages and had difficulty finding their place in unfamiliar conditions. But when, after the achieved victory (I use this term in as relative a sense as I can), the Polish administration brought hysteria to the city with terror, repressions, and disrespect, they conducted themselves precisely like an intruder, an aggressor, the conqueror of a strange city, like a blind barbarian, deaf to Lviv's primeval polyphony. And that is why they lost this city. The sorrow of the victorious – that is one unavoidable result of any victory.

But now we're heading into forbidden realms, further and further from culture.

As you can see, I did not keep my promise to talk about what unites. Maybe, I'll at least try to rescue this situation with a worthy conclusion?

The concept of an indivisible culture is not always convincing. The culture of the North and the culture of the South, the culture of the East and the culture of the West (let us also note that the Northeast and the Southwest also exist, and that they have their opposites, all with unlimited nuances) are concepts that are as unclear as they are divisive. Only though the grace of He Who Dispenses Geography, can something occasionally be combined with something else. And, at that, for a rather silly reason – for example, because of a watershed between two Sea basins. And it is because of that, that precisely here and now, at the end of the century and of the millennium, we have the wonderful opportunity to be passengers on one of those ships that floats, as it seems to us, in a generally predictable direction. Maybe it is actually an ark, in which, as was always the case in old, eclectic Lviv, we have been assembled to rescue a pair of every animal. Perhaps, other ship metaphors would work as well – drunken ship, ship of fools, ship of death. Or maybe, as Roth put it – a city of erased borders, a flowing Trieste, a wandering Lviv, Lwów, Lvov, Lemberg, Leopolis, Singapore.

1994

Carpathologia Cosmophilica

TRANSLATED BY MARK ANDRYCZYK

An attempt at fictitious regional studies
It is hard to believe but scientists confirm that in the distant past the Carpathians were
at the bottom of a sea. In the mountains the remains of sea creatures can be found:
sea shells, sea lilies, etc.

Elementary school nature studies textbook

1

Sea shells, sea lilies, and, also, tridacna, whale whiskers, polyps, pow-
dery fish skeletons, fossil vertebrae and fins, jaws of water creatures
that have not yet been studied by science and, of course, the carcasses
of the casualties of sunken ships (ribs, masts, sometimes only tattered
ropes and sails) covered with grasses and bird nests – all this visible
evidence of the Carpathians' maritime past accompanies anyone who
dares to travel upon the Chornohora mountain range along the Romanian border, with the damp paradise of Southern Pokuttia and Northern
Bukovyna, famous for its tobacco leaves and inedible grapes, behind
them, and, in front of them – only an old Austrian military road and
a row of enticing snowy peaks, the names of which, together with the
names of the adjacent valleys and dells, invoke endless chains of linguistic and acoustic associations: Drahobrat, Pip Ivan, Petros, Turkul,
Dantsyzh, Gadzhyna, Rebra, Shpytsi, Rozshybenyk, Hoverlia . . .

Travelling along the bottom of the non-existing sea, using only the
contours of the mountains, abandoned trenches, and machine-gun cartridges scattered in the grass to orient yourself, on the sixth day (in
other versions – in the sixth hour) of the journey you can finally get
close to the ruins of the largest of the forsaken vessels. But you must

avoid the dead waters of the lake with the woman's name Marichaika (a few of my acquaintances in Lviv, inexplicably call it Chaika-Mariia, which means Seagull Mary), on the shores of which all travellers, without exception, have nightmares with such indecipherable, yet worrying, symbolism that the only possible explanation could be that it is a powerful psychic-energy vortex, a space-time cluster, an astral-abyssal collapse. Local inhabitants explain this phenomenon by saying that the dreams of the drowned Mariia (Marichaika) wander in the lake environs, unable to find a place of rest. Anybody who dares to sleep above the motionless-black surface of the lake is destined to participate in these dispossessed reflections. And far from every wanderer has successfully returned from them: some of them remain *there*, at the bottom of awakened and arisen archetypes.

So we won't stop at this risky place but will continue our journey through the increasing Alpine landscape to, as has already been planned, the grandest of the dead ships. It stands before us like the fortress of fortresses, the materialized fancy of, let's say, Dino Buzzati, its fortification walls and towers recall a different world, an almost alien one, here, not far from the dell with the half-Romanian (Thracian) name Dzembronia.

This is a special relic of interwar architecture, a part of that mythical Lviv-Warsaw-Vienna-Paris vector, about which only rumours and assumptions circulate. This is a building and a structure, a dwelling, a workshop, a citadel, an academy, a library, halls for conferences, dances and gymnastics, a salon, a pool, an engine room, a restaurant, a power station, a boiler room, a line of pantries as well as a cellar and innumerable other quirky rooms with doors that are always closed, it's an ark, it's a complex. It's the complex of Europe, here, in its farthest territory at the border with Non-Europe, in the exact centre of Europe.

This was a former observatory, that is, a place for observing, for contemplation, for peering into and watching – perhaps angels, perhaps comets. Today one can find shelter from passing mountain rains behind its walls. The persistent odour of excrement and old rags will never be aired out, even by sixteen mountain valley breezes, which constantly dance within these walls because of holes and gaps – both in a metaphorical and in a literal sense. Travellers build campfires in the middle of the halls and corridors. The remains of the parquet floor are pretty good for burning – locals have known this provocative truth for a rather long time – that's why we're not really talking about the parquet floor per se, or about the light walnut panelling on the walls, or about the faded beech shelving in the library, but truly about "remains." It's hard to say what happened to the telescopes and all other kinds of astrophysical tools. It's doubtful that Poland managed to evacuate them in September 1939. Perhaps later, under Moscow, they were taken somewhere to the Caucasus region, to the Tian Shan or Pamir Mountains. Because Russia had little use for Carpathian observatories, having directed its fate towards much higher heights and even brazenly giving them its own lofty romantic names, such as, for example, Peak of Communism.

Although, Russia really is far away from it, and it almost doesn't exist.

Instead, there are Planeteers,[1] a special form of magicians and prophets, connected to every cosmic phenomenon through myriad invisible and painful currents. Isn't it they who created this field, this vacant land, this hole of emptiness? Isn't it through their efforts that this forbidden zone was created, this ruin, this whispering wind in nocturnal observatory corridors: "you can't come in? . . ."

The poet who first casually rhymed "Kosmach"[2] with "Cosmos" was correct a thousand times over.

2

Bukovyna, Pokuttia, the Hutsul region and the Maramureṣ region, Ciscarpathia and then also Transcarpathia, Transylvania, Potyssia, Podunavia – are all territories that, in one way or another, belong to the makeup of the Eastern Carpathians. Taras Prokhasko, my friend and writer-biosoph (and in his recent physical personification, a popular bartender in the Gartenberg Passage), nailed it when he called it "a structure-myth, beyond which destruction does not tread." Beyond, to the West – I specify the direction of his, perhaps, somewhat idealized, view.

This structure, regardless of its apparent location in a certain geographical centre, always was a border, an edge, a neighbourhood of an empire, a neighbourhood of culture and civilization. Roman coins, consistently found in Gothic tombs during the burrowing of tunnels and gas lines, dated to the time of Trajan and later, allow the more educated local inhabitants to claim, with a drink in hand, that their ancestors were citizens of one of the Roman empires (although not necessarily the Holy one). It is here, along the Carpathian line that the Latin and Byzantine worlds were demarcated, which can be seen through the demarcation of Western and Eastern rites. While Ottoman skulls, dug up every Spring in the fields of Khotyn, recall not only the unbearable decay of existence but also the incomprehensible cheapness and variety of today's market in Chernivtsi, which is so densely packed with all kinds of goods from Turkey that the amount of collected spoils of a Philippe de Mézièrez or the Ukrainian Hetman Hamaliya could never measure up to it.

As we can see, it wasn't only the Danube and the Neva monarchies that were responsible for the division ensured by this structure-universal – this division never really abated. Although the above-mentioned museum machine-gun cartridges lying in the trenches, overgrown with various mountain-valley grasses, do provide the fullest picture of the clash of the geopolitical interests of these two formations in particular. Actually, after their fall, this arch, this Cyrillic "C" flipped inversely, which itself demonstrates the idea of "vicinity," still remained a place of crossing vectors and influences, but now actively propagated by other, young, post-imperial countries and fiefdoms. But then came the giants in army boots, who filled the local wells with bodies of people they had shot in the back of the head, and in doing so, planted a bomb in its foundation that blew up exactly half a century later in the golden September of 1989, in a time of exhumations, wakes, re-burials, and the march of three hundred thousand people.

But we can suppose (the freedom of this genre fully allows for this) that, over the years, the influences of a completely different form dominated here. Not the visible and palpable influences of empires, armies, police, and politicians, but the secret influences of cosmic bodies and occult knowledge, taken in the past, for example, from India. But – as I like to stress – "not from that India that we know as a friendly country." But from a somewhat imagined, an unreal India, one for which the word "Rakhmanian"[3] is appropriate.

3

According to ancient Ukrainian beliefs, India is not really a peninsula and not really a mainland, it's more like an Island, which lies somewhere in the Ocean. The Island of India is inhabited by Rahmans[4] – rather unfortunate beings, who don't have calendars and don't know when Easter will take place. Thus, sitting on the shores of the Ocean, they meditate in anticipation. In anticipation of eggshells.

After Easter breakfast, the eggshells must be tossed into the nearest river or stream. Flowing down together with the water, the eggshells, without fail, end up in the Prut River, and from there, in the Danube, which is really just another name for the Nile. From the Danube, the path of the eggshells lies across the seas to the edge of the world. Caught and led by the warm streams, on the tenth Friday of their journey, the eggshells wash up to the shores of India. In this manner the Rahmans find out that Easter has arrived and they begin celebrating their, Rahmanian, Easter.

A long time ago, maybe seven and a half thousand years ago, that is, not long after the world was separated from the clouds and water, one of the Rahmanian tribes left India on boats and flying carpets. Today it is difficult to determine the reasons for this flight – it could have just as easily been a dimming of the mind or a mystic enlightenment. Abandoning the island, the escapees took almost all their secret knowledge with them – in sacks, in bags, and in their pockets. They didn't have books and didn't need them, because they knew all the main incantations and curses by heart. Among other important things, the stolen knowledge involved, first and foremost, the true counting of time, cause-effect columns and stratifications, the ability to read the past and predict the future based on palm readings, arranging chandeliers in a room or lights in the sky, the art of dressing a bear, hypnotizing children, and forging metals with heat.

The descendants of the Rahmans invented the violin and gold teeth. They didn't appear in the Eastern Carpathians until the Late Middle Ages, when King Karpo Dimwitsky, who had a propensity for alcohol and philanthropy let them through all four gates into his summer capital Chortopil, where they immediately set up a camp on the centre square, together with trained bears and countless children. That afternoon, stolen chickens and vegetables flowed to the Rahmanian tents in unremitting rivers and the inhabitants of Chortopil winced from the first fortunes they heard . . .

. . . This winter, they failed to leave our city. They always used to appear before spring, they would *arrive* in dirty red diesel local trains from warmer flatlands past the Carpathians, spread themselves out in streets and courtyards, filling the barely warmed air with nervousness, with playing cards and with a mix of Hungarian-Romanian-Slovak-Slovenian-Old Church Slavic-Ukrainian-Ruthenian[5]-Russian-Tarabarian and some other (maybe Sanskrit?) sounds, with this almost senseless mixture that has only one purpose – letting in fog and driving in gloom. And also, perhaps, saving myths. Because it is they, the tamers of bears and policemen, who were, are, and will always be the loyalist citizens of the non-existing Central Europe, its fictitious society, this

Rahmanian confederation, citizens of all the world's patchwork monarchies and town republics.

So then, this winter they did not leave our city. Usually, they would leave with the first autumn snows, when living in the squares became unsuitable not only for birds, but even for them. But this winter, they did not leave. Perhaps they received some secret signs.

I hope that they correctly interpreted them.

4

"I made it my goal to correctly grasp the essence of the *astrology* of all civilized peoples in ancient and modern times and after ten years of exhausting research, which really took its toll on me, I've finally achieved a result that greatly exceeded my expectations, so, with complete courage, I can confirm that a person's fate, his future, without question, can be studied, but only if those ridiculous requirements utilized by medieval astrologers are discarded, and, if instead, one remains within the bounds of that reasonableness with which people are outlined by the very imperfection of their nature." This was written on the Day of the Phoenix, that is, 21 March 1883 AD by the poetic and exotic character from the city of Czernowitz, a retired officer of the Austrian army, combatant in the 1859 expedition in northern Italy, surveyor, pharmacist, admirer of patriotic criticism, the "Bukovynian Nightingale" and "Carpathian Shevchenko" in one person, a Hutsul[6] with Polish roots inherited from his father, the romantic, the populist and Planeteer Dominik Ferdinand Osyp Yuri cavalier von Fedkovych de Hordynsky.[7]

Ten years of life turned into ten thousand pages of an astrological treatise, written in a specifically Bukovynian version of the classic High German language. (That was probably the language spoken by Olha Kobylianska. While Paul Celan already spoke, without a doubt, a different language.) Based on photos that have faded over time, Fedkovych, although he totally had Viennese features, always walked around in a Hutsul vest. Although it is quite possible that he never really walked around in it, but just put it on for the photo. And, maybe, consistent with his emulation of Shevchenko, cavalier de Hordynsky may have seen this clothing as the perfect Bukovynian equivalent of Shevchenko's sheepskin coats and hats.

But then again in Chernivtsi-Czernowitz of that time, located on the main trade route from Lviv to Iași: (today, as has already mentioned, from Lviv to Istanbul), there existed such a joyful ethnic mix of people that it was almost impossible to astonish anyone with your clothing.

Fedkovych was recognizable from afar. Every day, a waiter he knew from the inexpensive restaurant "The Green Hunter," which was located across the street from him, would bring him a carafe of Slivovitz and serve it together with the tray, right into his window. They say the restaurant's owner gave it to him for free – Fedkovych would occasionally draw up horoscopes for him and his family free of charge.

At the beginning of the century, an introduction (not even eight typed pages) to his aforementioned treatise was included in his Collected Works. The gothic outline of Fraktur letters of his text begged comparison to other popular works of that time (Nietzsche, Zarathustra, the Aryan symbols for fire, the swastika, *und so weiter*). Ptolemy's great map of the stars in the heavens, which the German Romantics so excitedly called "das Firmament," would also fit here. But the exceedingly progressive publishers treated the treatise completely in line with their positivist world view: seeing it as a strange turbulence in Fedkovych's not-too-sober mind (which once was called "lost his marbles"). They were not even swayed by the iron-like logic and artillery-like accuracy of the lecture. Here's an example: "So far as everything in the macro-world is governed by strong, unwavering, mathematically and accurately calculated laws, it also applies to the micro-world, to the individual, in our case, a person. Subordinated to one and the same dependence, they influence one another, but according to their size, strength, and power. Since these three main potencies are irrefutable, and Existence is also inexorably subordinated to mathematic laws, thus, in that manner, the mutual influences of the macro-world and the micro-world can be calculated with mathematical accuracy. And since the fate of a person is just the sum of the influences of the universum (the macro-world) on a person (the micro-world), then these mutual influences can be calculated both in the past and in the future."

It seems that the publishers were not impressed with the following particular biographical moment of intrigue either: "in his youth he [the author] was told his future by a certain astrologer and it has all come true to this day, thus, this is what led him to multi-year, tireless research, which really took a toll on him." And the following sensational assertion had no effect – implying that "the author has the right to think that he discovered a key, which had been lost in the past and had been used by ancient Egyptian astrologers as they opened the doors to the future."

But how did he get hold of this key? We ask today, following Fedkovych himself, who, however, replies most comprehensively: "This needs to remain a mystery."

Yes, this needs to remain a mystery.

Nevertheless: how did he get a hold of that key? From what Northern Italy did he bring this priceless trophy? From what astrologer, wandering rogue, or two-bit scoundrel, disguised as a barber, could he have received this rare knowledge, be it Rahmanian, Indian, Egyptian? Or maybe it came to him as a vision, partly coded in Hutsul dreams and overthrown archetypes? This wild structure, this fusion, this mix of plants, languages, drinks, and feelings, called the Carpathians, wasn't that what caused a stormy, cosmic reaction, the result of which everything, and I mean e v e r y t h i n g, is revealed and shows through, like a sign on a palm – you just need to read it?!

The last chords of the treatise's introduction are as eclectic as they are ecstatic. The demiurge defeats the surveyor. The alchemist rises above the pharmacist. The free trembling of essence and substance gives birth to a pathetic quivering of lungs and diaphragms: "Glory to you, Eternal, to Your eyes, Soul of the Universe, Man of time immortal, Keeper of the Phoenix, who shines the holy onto life, halleluiah to You to the heavens!

And if it is Your will, send it to Your servant, who preaches verity, in Your eternal verity for the good and devotion of the pious, You, who are the eternal verity and truth!

And you, the Only Begotten Son, who holds Seven Stars in his right hand, and whose lips – a double-edged sword, help me with all Your might to deliver the word to the unworthy that You are the Alpha and Omega, the beginning and the end! You who have no beginning and no end!"

I'm not sure if the actual treatise has been preserved. Perhaps the Keeper of the Phoenix did not find it necessary to resurrect it, the treatise, from the ashes. Because manuscripts really do burn and who knows this better then arsonists?

But, nonetheless, we received something in inheritance. An abandoned observatory, a gaze upward. Something not quite clear, some kind of vertical orientation, nothing more.

It seems like we're listening to the music of the spheres. Or the opposite – to Hutsul music.

5

It isn't easy to find music in this world that is earthier than that of the Hutsuls. On the level of biological tension, physicality, sex, and death, perhaps only Romanian music can compare. Or gypsy. Or the music of the Gorals.[8] Or of the Hungarians. Or of the Slovaks. Or of the Lemkos.

I believe that Hutsul music still does exist although it may be gone by tomorrow. Most of us won't even notice this, first and foremost the Hutsuls themselves. Today, many of them are completely satisfied with not just Madonna but with Masha Rasputina.[9] The empire of Russian pop music has not given up an inch of its territory. Its border, as it was earlier, stretches out west to Chop and Mostyska. This empire of kiosks dictates its will, more accurately, it wills itself. Hutsul music degenerates into kitsch. The Central Europe of Kosiv and Rakhiv gets washed away into Eurasia. A jumping off place is created from which the unified, or more accurately, the infected, "citizens of the CIS" constantly move West. And they ask to listen to Masha Rasputina.

And what are we left with? And what are we to do?

Music is not the only reality in the hazy structure of Central Europe. Music gives sense to conversations about unity and uniqueness. It lies beyond all chronic conflicts and stereotypes. Its plots are wandering, its characters universal.

Of course, this music would never exist if it were not for the Carpathians. Perhaps we can also say the opposite: there would be no Carpathians if it were not for this music. Everything else is just mutual pretensions, attacks, seizures, assimilation. Everyone has wronged everyone else. Survival at the expense of the weaker, the sucking out of raw materials, cheap labour, mountain robbery, severed heads displayed at crossroads, religious conflicts, and a basic, drunken, blood fest. To construct some kind of society on a foundation such as this (other than a mafia society) is, perhaps, as difficult as rewriting history again, and even the only magnificent piece of this history, the utopia of the Danube monarchy, won't seem so justifiable. The most pragmatic of politicians have already understood the true state of things.

So what are we to do? Go on mountain excursions and record folklore? Watch for the heavenly bodies of angels though the holes of the tents of unused observatories? Look for old treatises, rebirth astrology? Cleanse the principle elements of culture of cause-effect stratifications? Save Hutsul music? Or, maybe, wait for a large arrival of eggshells from across the ocean?

As a special meta-science of the future, carpathology has not yet developed finalized answers to these and other fundamental questions. So this is all we know for sure.

The Carpathians are a large clamp holding together parts of existence that are prone to chaotic crawling. The Carpathians comprise a large seismic force, a zone of special energetic possibilities and tensions. The Carpathians divide in a terrestrial sense but unite in a cosmic one. Probably, both senses are equally necessary and definitive. And if that is so, then this is the start of a dialogue. It's important that it have no end. For everything else it is worth depending on Him, Who has no beginning or end.

1996

Time and Place, or My Final Territory

TRANSLATED BY MARK ANDRYCZYK

1

Inviting me to participate in this gathering,[1] Yaroslav Hrytsak informed me that my presentation has to be a voice "in defence of postmodernism" and, here's one more quote – "postmodernism with a human face." There was nothing I could do but accept this proposition and take on this not-very-thankful assignment. It seems that the precedent itself of the appearance of such an apologetic need demonstrates that there is a certain nervousness that has been sown in our intellectual circles over the last ten years – that is, from the moment that this slippery concept was put into circulation. And, truthfully, the time has finally come when only the lazy or dead do not criticize postmodernism in our lands. Personally, I don't consider myself to be lazy and I certainly am alive so I would happily join the side attacking. Moreover, because, it seems to me, the approach of the attackers is clear, steadfast, and promises to be victorious. Once I tried to systematize and list all (or, at least, the most often used) attacks on postmodernism and it turned out that:

1) It is concerned almost exclusively with quotation, it creates collages and montages, it is a parasite living off texts that have already been written;
2) It renders play for the sense of play an absolute, excluding the living authenticity of creation, of suffering, of the soulful and the spiritual, as well as the dignity of narration and super-narration from discourse;
3) It compromises any belief in the Mission of Literature (regardless of what is understood by that); in other words, postmodernism – is the death of literature;

4) It applies irony to everything in the world, including irony itself, discarding ethical systems (actually, now just "pieces of ethical systems") and didactic aims (more accurately, "the echoes of these aims") of any sort;

5) It combines the para-individual author's "I" with all other authors' worlds; thus, postmodernism is once again – death, the death of the author as a creator of his own individual authorial world;

6) It uses a "carnival" (really just a post-carnival) mask to hide from any responsibility to Those Nearby and That Which is Nearby;

7) It brazenly experiments with language(s), it mechanically accumulates methods and means and their combinations, thus, for the third time – "with heavy heart and boredom we share the sad news";

8) It slavishly kowtows to the virtual, to multimedia abysses and brutes, it wants art to be under the control of electronic empires and for its soul to be forever buried in its interspiderweb;

9) It toys with mass culture, it demonstrates bad taste, vulgarity, it does not disregard "sex, sadism, and violence";

10) It ruins hierarchy, it shifts foundations, it removes significance, it clears boundaries, it puts words, and then existence itself, in quotation marks, it makes an already chaotic life even more chaotic, it uses irony, quotes, it makes collages and montages … well, we've already said that.

It that case, all you can say about postmodernism is that it is

a) agnostic, agonistic, ambivalent, American, anemically ill
b) "a boundlessly open dead end," barren, bi- (and more) sexual
c) collage, conformist, consumption
d) discursively defecating
e) egalitarian, entropic, eclectic, epigonic
f) fragmented, feminized, Fellini-ized
g) gutturally pretentious
h) hermaphrodite, hetero-semantic, homoerotic
i) imitative, impotent, intertextual, incestuous
j) juvenile, junky
k) kooky
l) lobotomized
m) mannerist, mimicking
n) neo-necrophilic, numbing, nasty
o) ontologically marginal
p) pathologically plump
q) queer

r)   recreational, reminiscent
s)   stuffed, situational
t)   transvestite
u)   uranic
v)   varietal, vulgarizing
w)   whiney, whimsical, wishy-washy
x)   xenogenetic, X-rayish
y)   yesterdayish
z)   zigzagging, zombie-inducing

In addition, it is characterized as "postcolonial" and "post-totalitarian," but this doesn't really explain anything, especially in our case.

Also, it is "nothing."

Sometimes they say that something similar had been seen before: the Alexandria epoch, the autumn of the Middle Ages, fin-de-siècle decadence, any exhausted/supersaturated cultural formation. This can confidently be tied to the end of a certain intermediate chronological countdown, for example, to the boundary of the century.

Some people are inclined to believe that postmodernism begins where – forgive me the tautology – an author's auto-reflection begins. The place where text stops being a means and becomes the goal – that is where the borders and posts of postmodernism are found. The place where the author forgets about message and falls into self-admiration, the place where the author-narcissist appears, that is where the end begins. And because that is the way it has always been, postmodernism too has always been, and thus, has never been.

I am lost among all this variety. All I can do is search for solely personal traits and definitions. I look around me – where am I?

2

I live in a part of the world that has been distrusted and disregarded since time immemorial. That part of the world is called Galicia. Perhaps that is why there is nothing else I can do but call myself a postmodernist. This, of course, is a joke, just not a very funny one.

There are regions that are real and those that are whole, even in their state of ruin and in their monstrosity. Galicia is completely fake, sewed together with the white threads of pseudo-historical fantasies and by the intrigues of politicos. Those who say that Galicia is just the one-hundred-and-fifty-year-old invention of a few Austrian ministers are correct a thousand times over. The preciously sweet obsession of certain conspiring strategists, who, at one time decided chimerically to extend Europe a bit farther to the East. They weren't successful in creating Europe there but, instead, a kind of buffer was formed, a kind of "sanitary zone." Poor Ivan Franko fell for their mystifications, and this is from where all his bad luck stems, all his disoriented Sisyphean activity.

From the perspective of, let's say, Polissia, this land looks like a caricature. Because Polissia, that cosmic, pagan cradle, the basin of the Prypiat and the Desna Rivers with the Aryan purity of its roots and the Derevlianian clarity of its wells, with its definitive genetic-cultural codes, with its most-ancient of folklores, epos, dialects, lakes, peat, gothic pine trees, with traps for animals and people, with wounded wolves, Polissia is the national substratum, it is Ukraine's Chernobyl choice, it is genuineness itself, it is pure authenticity and honesty, the punitive expedition of the messiah Onoprienko[2] along the train tracks and highways. Polissia is slowness and dreariness, it is time that has almost stopped, it is the crawling communist eternity that has surrounded the despised, corrupt, and tormented-a-hundredfold Kyiv,[3] it is deep black Ukrainianness.

From the perspective of Polissia, Galicia does not exist, that is, it does, but that fact is useless. Galicia is non-Ukraine, it's some kind of geographic add-on, a Polish hallucination. Galicia is very much like a mannequin, like a doll, blown up everywhere and it always tries to thrust its non-Ukrainian will, which has been distilled somewhere in dark Zionist laboratories, upon Ukraine. Galicia has no epos, it has always been ruled by anecdotes, and foul ones at that. Indeed, it is a rootless expanse, suitable for all kinds of wandering tribes – Armenians, Gypsies, Karaites, and Hassids are from here. Galicia is the town-strewn fatherland of Freemasonry and Marxism. Galicia is hypocritical and fake, it's an odiferous menagerie overfilled with vipers and chimeras, only a mongrel such as Bruno Schulz, or any one of those little kafkas from Stanislaviv, are possible in Galicia, and, if you're not a mongrel, like Stefanyk, for example, then there's nothing for you to do other than relentlessly to get drunk in the first godforsaken hole you meet. "By the way, there are more geniuses in Ivano-Frankivsk today than there are in Moscow" – the acerbic Igor Klekh, also a Galician, and also a genius, says ironically from Moscow in his latest book.

An ironic tone is as suitable here as ever. Galicia is completely ironic and immoral, which explains the eternal perfidy and adaptation, the permanent Uniate quality, children sold to America. Galicia is showy and shallow, like detachable collars, obsequiousness, comical bowing to all sides, kissing of hands and of one's superiors with the still-lingering, uncouth smacking of lips, it is endless and sleepy conversations about Europe, Europa, Evropa after lunch, about what it means to be European, the definition of European, the role of Europe, European culture and cuisine, about the path to Europe, about the idea that "and we too are in Europe" – and meanwhile all of Galicia's so-called spiritual production put together can fit in a medium size Lviv suitcase. All that Galicia is capable of doing is to try so much to be like Europe, which hasn't been able to do anything on its own now for quite a while (Spengler said this way back when!). Galicia is a plagiarism, and an especially pathetic one because the plagiarizer chose to plagiarize the deadest of all possible objects.

And the rest is just coffee, homemade liqueurs, cakes and pastries, dictatorial housewives, napkin embroidery, as well as marmalades and jams, traditional embroidered cloths, kilim rugs, bad taste and kitsch, in other words, the blooming of Galician philistine existence to its fullest.

From the perspective of Polissia, Galicia isn't just pitiful – it's postmodern.

But I have a different perspective. More accurately, I don't have one because I am here, inside, this is my territory, this is my distrusted and disregarded world, the fortification walls around it have long since been knocked down, the moats have been filled with historical junk and cultural garbage, some smashed porcelain of sorts, Havarechchyna black ceramics, Hutsul tiles, my only line of defence is me myself, but I don't have any other choice but to defend this piece, this patch, these patches that are tearing at the seams every which way.

3

They are tearing at the seams, but I try to pull them in, sew them together, if only with the white threads of my own versions and inventions, and here I need another territorial ephemeron, some kind of geographical ghost, a parallel reality, one that was in fashion just yesterday but that is pretty much spewed out at intellectual receptions today – Central Europe. No, not Europe as such, not its twilight, but a Centre, more accurately, an East, because in Europe, paradoxically, East is where the Centre is. Central Europe, the child of Kundera, Miłosz, and Konrád: a strange substance made up only of ideas, senses, mystifications, the

American invention of a few disgruntled dissidents. We stand at the threshold of its final disappearance, just as soon as the Poles, together with the Slovak-Hungarians, are accepted into NATO, and thus into the West, to "the real Europe," and Ukraine – into a renewed Slavic federation; just as soon as all the locks are locked up tight on the Western borders of our second most important Soviet republic, just as soon as the old border guards return to their fortified posts with young, ambitious watchdogs lacking muzzles in tow.

Thus, it does not exist, this Central Europe, more accurately, it almost doesn't exist, in the same way that Galicia is almost not a part of it. And all that exists is "almost," the complete territory of postmodernism. Which, it seems has nothing to do with Lyotard, Derrida, or Said, or maybe, in fact, completely has to do with them, but that's not what I'm talking about.

What I am talking about is that it is here, in this territory, that I see certain indicators of what I understand to be "post-modern," that is "after-modern" – what came after modernism, with its natural striving for the modern, for the new, in synch with the times, a striving, actually, that was interrupted brutally, from outside, by blood, ashes and world wars, but also by dictatorships, concentration camps, and massive ethnic cleansings – in such a manner, in this part of the world, modernism was halted, killed, and cut off at the knees, all versions of modernism – Vienna (the standard), Prague, Cracow, Lviv, Drohobych, after which an after-modern wasteland came, a massive hollowness with an endlessly open potential, a nothingness that promises a lot.

I also see this "postmodern" as a not-yet-fully formed, but already noticeable, after-totalitarianism. And I see this as a constant neo-totalitarian danger, an amoeba that can take over everyone in space and the entire space itself. Historically, modernism developed at the same time as totalitarian political systems did, more than one of its black squares was a materialized temptation of the "new man." Postmodernism comes after totalitarianism, it is amorphous, chimerical, it is a beast that suits a transitional, disoriented state, destroying a former axis, leaving only fragments of the vertical, the bright future cleverly standing in for the apocalypse.

There exists another dimension of the "postmodern" in our part of the world. It is the factor of multiculturalism, which is mentioned a lot, often and correctly – but, in reality, this multiculturalism is projected towards the past, it existed earlier, now it is post-multiculturalism, we have only the traces, only tracks.

We have ruins (of castles, of holy places, of factories, of bridges, of observatories, most of the ruins are cemeteries, because there is nothing easier than taking over the dwellings of those who have fled, but who will tend to strangers' graves?). We have ruins, these are signs of "the stratification of cultures" and also of "the stratification of anti-cultures," this is imposed landscape collages, this is true postmodernism, playing with the bricks of existence, but it is not we who are the players in this game.

We have quotations – lost languages, scrolls, dialects, burned manuscripts, fragments of poems – fragments of a lost wholeness, but it is not we who juggle these fragments. We have the prevalence of mythologies. Because in this part of the world, mythology compensates for history, family stories are more important, and much more believable here than history books. In fact, history here itself is nothing more than a version of mythology.

Finally, I also see my "postmodern" as the provincial, the marginal – in the sense that Central Europe never could be, and never wanted to be, the centre (which didn't stop it from constantly impregnating the centre with its live sperm, usurping systems of values, forming streams of consciousness, but I'm not going to talk about all those blissful upstarts now, all those the warhols and chagalls), because "Central Europe – it's a special state of the soul, a special way of looking at the world," my friend Krzysztof Czyżewski says. And I will dare to add: it is a provincial space where everyone knows that they actually belong in the centre, because the centre is simultaneously nowhere and everywhere, and that is why from the heights and the depths of your own office you can easily see everything, including New York or some Moscow. And here it is – the absence of any axes, here is the human chaos of existence, "knots of connections" everywhere, the vertical with the horizontal and vice versa.

And this is what I like most of all.

4

Actually, I couldn't care less what they call it. Postmodernism? Okay, that's fine. Something else is more important.

There exists a call to life and there exists a call to death, and I react to them as well as I can. I am pulled to one side, and then to the other, something is happening to me, I notice changes within me, but, fortunately, I can't control them. Moreover – I can't handle them. All I can do is write. All I can do is hope that in my writing I am equal to my reactions – I don't strive for anything else. In the end, it is not that important how they name, qualify, or classify what comes out of me ... even if nothing comes out.

But I will never agree with the idea that everything has already taken place in this world.

Perhaps it is that indicator in particular that allows me to think that postmodernism (fine, let's call it "postmodernism"!) – is where we have all found ourselves today, it's a circumstance of time and place, from which we cannot escape, a territory "between" and "within," a dependent-on-no-one inter-civilizational, but also super-civilizational space, the central hole of Europe, a tectonic shift, an abyss, the lost commentary on Galicia, in fact, it is Galicia itself, a gap between millennia, it's the trash of all of our downtowns, our memory, our hope, our solitude – you are left alone with tangled fragments, lines, words, with alcohol, with a fever, with slang and *surzhyk*,⁴ with all the languages of the world, with the one and only language, you are tortured by love, hate, sorrow, sex, you are stricken with all the world's human diseases and dreams, thoughts about death, about time and chaos, you are at least two thousand years old and you still have not written a single decent book.

They say to you "this is – postmodernism," you nod in response and again submerge yourself into anticipation – you are unlucky, this is a very vulnerable territory, this is reality itself, but it is yours.

1999

A Little Bit of Urban Studies

TRANSLATED BY MARK ANDRYCZYK

1

Any contemporary geographic map indicates that the city of Lviv lies North and a bit West from the city where I live. The city of Kyiv, on the other hand, is North and a great deal East. However, for residents of Ivano-Frankivsk who are travelling, as one of the results of World War II, both cities are located seemingly along a single line. The reason for this – the ruined (I'm not sure any more whether it was by the Germans or by the Russians) train bridge over the Dnister River. As a result, passenger train #203 Ivano-Frankivsk-Kyiv, disregarding geography, sets off, according to its final destination point, on a North-West deviation. It arrives in Lviv after the first three hours of its journey, in the early evening. Almost everyone gets off onto the platform, still rather fresh and relaxed. Those who went at it right after they departed Frankivsk restock their alcohol supplies and train station snacks. Others also usefully take advantage of this break – they pick up or pass along packages, meet up briefly with friends, enjoy the fresh air outside the train car. Almost twelve hours left to Kyiv, which isn't so bad.

I've been travelling regularly on this line, Frankivsk-Lviv-Kyiv, since around the time I was seventeen. I don't doubt that I've travelled over those tracks the equivalent of the Earth's circumference several times. But this line doesn't just exist for me in the realm of space.

It also contains a temporal dimension. Lviv is the first city in the world I ever moved to. It was the beginning of July, five a.m., I could hardly wait for the train, covered with the dew of the train station grass – not the Kyiv, but Rakhiv, train. It had recently passed through the mountains, evident not only by the remnants of frost on the train car roofs, but also by the great number of gypsies in all the train vestibules.

The image of the world formed a perfect totality. An incredibly slow, creaky train, the magnetic proximity of the Centre of Europe, Galicia beyond the windows, a four-hour tearing at the wound of anxiety, and finally – arrival: everything, including the trolleys, cobblestones, the pseudo-Gothic Elżbieta Cathedral next to the grossly neglected buildings on Horodotska Street, confirmed that the goal had been achieved (Europe! culture! freedom! joy!).

This ended up lasting for a while – for five years, longer even. That is why I sometimes feel justified in referring to my youth as a Lviv youth. I realize the seriousness of such a statement. Hundreds of thousands of people live in their time and place without realizing that, first of all, it is their youth and that, second of all, it is their Lviv youth. And most of all, I've never really been able to explain its particularities to an outsider, what is so unique about it. All I can come up with are some lilac bushes, a bottle of cheap booze consumed on High Castle, the panorama of old roofs and fortifications, and music, too, for example, Jethro Tull, but what of it?

This entire Lviv youth idea is not very convincing, I agree. But at least it is *something*, compared to my so-called Kyiv youth. Because that one is just a ghost that hovered over me as I was sleeping, for several years, fooling me and frightening me, blowing hangover-breath in my face, or, as a more radical *master of the word* might have worded it – a spiritual death.

That's why there's no sense remaining by it any longer.

2

But what about that Lviv youth?

First and foremost, it left a bitter aftertaste. That feeling is known as disappointment. It's a very good sense, incredibly fruitful, and deeply creative, according to authors of coming-of-age-stories that I know. Disappointment appears on that invisible border where the imagined meets the real. And that border truly is invisible, which is why disappointment can sometimes imperceptibly turn into satisfaction and vice versa.

The imagined city of Lviv lay on picturesque, green hills, completely preserving the architectonics and architecture of a, perhaps, medieval city. Clavichord music, or, at least, good sympho-rock, played non-stop from open windows, and girls with long hair and wreaths awaited me in the grass by fountains. In the imagined Lviv, only Ukrainian was spoken, with the exception of, perhaps, some old witches and female sorcerers speaking Latin or Greek. Also, everyone there knew the poetry of Antonych by heart, and wandering minstrels performed outdoor concerts. There was a system of tunnels and chambers below the city, filled with an endless supply of wine, gold, fabrics, and old tomes. In general, this was a city of never-ending mystery and its women, plants, and rain all had this scent of mystery. I knew that Lviv's river had been buried underground but, real, Atlantic eels lived in it, for the city de facto was situated in the world's Atlantic zone, perhaps even at the shore of a sea.

The real Lviv consisted of about 90 per cent hideous suburbs and new building projects. The collection of industrial territories, the chaos of factory rail yards, the monotonous residential zones of the 1970s and of later years, iron and concrete, structural building panels, a nasty stench, and the gnashing of teeth. The fatal helplessness of the city government to resolve issues with water rationing, the sewage system, transportation. Any music heard coming from a window would be Soviet pop music, the amount of Russian language heard in the city would be frighteningly high. And what was even worse was the fact that those who spoke Ukrainian were almost all rather dim-witted and lazy hicks. University students, with their looks, level of communication, and conduct were akin to graduates of a tech school for imbeciles. And the so-called national intelligentsia exhibited the wonders of submissiveness and servility, sublimating all of their Ukrainianness in plump physiques and embroidered shirts. Together, all of this formed the ugliest of all the forms of sovok[1] that I know – Ukr-sovok.

That is why I'm left only with a belief in the existence of some kind of parallel, secret Lviv. Occasionally, that city would send me signals about its existence. Sometimes in the form of a shadow – in the galleries of the old city musty from dirt – of a certain character, who was not from here and not from this time, but instead was from a country all of whose inhabitants have flown the coop. Sometimes – news about one political process or another, an off-beat art exhibition, the rock-opera "Stepan Bandera" or the gathering of flower children from the Holy Orchard. Now and then – the appearance on the horizon of a completely real Dem, Valeriy Demianyshyn. A showing of a Tarkovsky film, a stroll through the Lychakiv Cemetery, a midnight jaunt into darkness along the hills of High Castle. All of this could serve to confirm the existence of that other Lviv. In the most catastrophic times of youth I was able to come at night to Rynok Square with an already opened bottle or without one.

What's most interesting is that just as my Lviv youth ended, I found myself right in the crosshairs of that secret Lviv, in its thick atmosphere – saturated with wine, sleeplessness, love, and dampness. I was able to convince myself that all my imagining was not in vain. And although the Vuiky no longer played, Kalynets no longer wrote, and Chubai[2] was no longer alive, I nonetheless felt a connection with the mysteries of that city.

And it was then that I was forced to return to my native city, scribbling this disenchantment with my life all over my notebooks and preparing for the entirely likely need to resist the insanity of the rest of my life.

It's bad that almost none of the imagined came to fruition. It's good that things played out the way that they did.

3

It's good that I don't live in Kyiv. It's good that this was just a nightmare of youth. That is why I don't know that city. Maybe I'm just conjecturing about it. But for me, this city begins at six-thirty a.m., when I exit the train and hear – in my face and behind me – the foreboding calls of the Russian-speaking taxi drivers "Mushchina, taksi niedoroha!" ("Yo guy, cheap taxi here!").

The first characteristics of Kyiv, according to many of my acquaintances, is that it seems to be a non-Ukrainian city. First and foremost this is because of the language situation, which I think, beginning in 1991 or even in 1990, exists in the state of permanent pendulum movement in both – Ukrainian and Russian – directions. But it's not just this.

Kyiv, in general, exists in a zone of different, "non-Ukrainian," mental-psychological influences. The constant influx of absolutely prototypical Ukrainianness from far away, or nearby, towns and villages is unable to change Kyiv, the opposite occurs – Kyiv changes the Ukrainianness. The most perceptible manifestation of this is the completely mechanical nature of Kyiv's urban existence. Unlike all other European capitals, in Kyiv there is no moveable feast – regardless of all the formal popular gatherings that take place in the city. The massive movement of faceless streams of people, a mutual anxiety, isolation, an inclination towards clashing, aggression, the lack of improvisation, spiritual delight, and play with interrelations – all of these show the Kyivan populace to be a gigantic chaotic collection of people who don't know and have no need for one another. No, in Kyiv you won't notice that unbearable lightness of being of which there is so much of in Paris, Prague, Belgrade, or even New York. Existence is tricky and life is sticky, if I can allow myself a mindless rhyme. Occasionally, only soccer can stimulate an outward manifestation of a deeply hidden human face, but this is such a senseless and fleeting catalyst that it cannot really change anything.

My friend Yurko Pozayak,[3] it seems, may disagree with me. He is mindful of a very different Kyiv, of truly exotic enclaves, of an internal, hidden, town character, with its own real rhythms, codes, self-rule, and language, for example – the *Ievbaz*.[4] I don't so much believe him as in the fact that he needs to be believed. Otherwise we won't make it, one on one against this – no, not Moloch – mulch.

For me Kyiv is islands in the ocean, a tiny pinch of people, who live here, scattered over editorial rooms, recording studios, apartments, cafes – those who over years or even decades, unnoticed by others, resist the mechanical nature of Kyiv and remain living people. There are great distances between them, which can only be overcome with the help of the metro. In essence, my paths are movements from one bastion to another, thus, Kyiv is really ten or so miniature fortresses. Going outside remains very much undesirable and fatally dangerous, except, perhaps, to stock up on alcohol reserves. Monsters with twisted faces walk around saying something not entirely clear in their half-language.

Of all the roles in this world, the closest to me is that of a storyteller. And that means that language – and I mean language, not writing, but spoken language, is most important to me. No less important to me is to listen to others: how one speaks in this world and what he's *clamouring about*. During my many-hour, evening, and nighttime odysseys through *dives* and bars, I'm ready to listen to anyone – drunks chewed up by life, worn-out athletes and businessmen, male artists and female artists, joyful mafiosos, sentimental prostitutes, sons of bitches, daughters of bitches, all these people, sometimes mistakenly referred to as *the narod* (the people). I, the Patriarch of Bu-Ba-Bu, cannot live without this. This is normal, this is what always takes place in Frankivsk or in Lviv, and that's the way it has been in Cracow, Prague, and Berlin.

But in Kyiv this is almost impossible: my angels-friends save me from all chance encounters – danger lingers in such exchanges, in such venturing out, it's a horrible risk, it concludes, at best, with the cracking of a skull (I, a happy paranoid soul, can already see that Kyiv asphalt with my teeth spilled out onto it). There is an ocean of no-good around us, my friends say.

That is why, in Kyiv, writers only converse with other writers. Or, as they think, *they converse with God*. Because what else is there left to do?

4

It's good that I don't live in Lviv. In the years since I lived there, the water rationing issue, it seems, has not been resolved. However, in general, life in Lviv has lately become noticeably more pleasant: even in our current situation, which is chronically hostile to any private initiative, initiative itself has managed to somewhat affect the city's everyday life and landscape. But it's good that I don't live in Lviv, because I'm not overly concerned with something being pleasant.

Since the beginning of the 1990s, there has existed the idea that Lviv is decaying. This idea is supported simply by the external appearance of the city's ruin: the state of streets, buildings, the crumbling of balconies, rain gutters and building ornaments, the darkness, fog and cold, the courtyards strewn with feces and trash. Lviv was, literally, dying, having been transformed into one big train station, a place from which throngs of Commonwealth of Independent States people in rabbit-fur hats and track suits would set off across Ukraine's western border.

Simultaneously, Lviv was abandoned (and continues to be abandoned today) by many riders of Train #92. They're a category of people that are half-Kyivites and half-Lvivites. And now most of them have made their choice – at least temporarily – in favour of Kyiv. Lviv has visibly lost people that are young, talented, flexible, and smart. They like to blame the *idiots in city hall* for their choice, but a very much mercantile reason for such a migration is also clear to the naked eye. Kyiv awaited them with much higher salaries and dizzying careers (an individual possessing a higher education and a solid knowledge of the official state language could go to bed a budding journalist and wake up the next morning a vice-minister of something or other, or, at least his secretary, which are essentially one and the same thing). Some individuals coyly justified their move with the need to *somehow Ukrainianize Kyiv*, but it was customary, and maybe, proper, to laugh at such individuals.

Generally speaking, a certain vicious circle was drawn – Lviv is decaying because its best inhabitants are leaving town, and its best inhabitants are leaving town because Lviv is decaying.

But in reality, as later years demonstrated, Lviv didn't decay at all. It's true that, in a certain sense, it doesn't really progress. But that's because Lviv is conservative by nature. Lviv always maintains approximately the same number of bastards, crazies, patriots, citizens, townsfolk, bohemians, idiots, Russkies – all categories of inhabitants. That is, they remain in approximately consistent proportions. And this allows Lviv to remain true to itself, even in its temporarily discordant state.

5

"In Lviv they say that the poet K., it seems, is very angry with you," an exegete confessed some troublesome news, as always, to me. "That's because in Lviv, they always say," I responded to this.

In Lviv they say, it seems, that the daughter of Dr T. travelled to America to give birth there. In Lviv they say, it seems, that the dentist Dr S. removes gold crowns from dead bodies. In Lviv they say, it seems, that E. is sleeping with B., and C. with P. In Lviv they say, it seems, that H. likes little boys. In Lviv they say, it seems, at Y.'s art opening, the sandwiches that were served had roach poison in them. In Lviv they say, it seems, that R. has gotten quite bald lately, and probably has taken a lover. In Lviv they say, it seems, that K-sky didn't show up for church last Sunday. In Lviv they say, it seems, This One bought a new house, That One bought a Riesenschnauzer, and That One Over There is Jewish. In Lviv they say.

In order to understand the importance of the *they say* factor for Lviv, it is worth multiplying its effect by the political and existential constraints of all previous epochs, especially the last one. By the atmosphere of denunciations, fabrications, and the imprisonment of souls. Yes, it is in Lviv that it was first said that, it seems, Dz. repented and abdicated, J. sold out, and J.C. got crucified.

It is because of this that the city was able to survive, preserving itself during the most difficult years. Lviv rumours and gossiping are a means for mutual support. Because true Lvivites are one big family, la familia, a mafia, where everyone supports one another with non-stop gossiping, interest, jealousy, hatred bordering on love, incessant attention. It's incredibly alive, this Lviv. No wonder it has a feline lineage.[5]

Lviv watches you, or rather, looks inside you, like Nietzsche's abyss.[6] You can't hide anything from it – it's a wonderful detector, a detective almost, and nothing can escape its gaze – not national betrayal, not plain old adultery, not even a little bit of cheating during a game of Bridge. But this is what is important: Lviv forgives everything. Because a family goes through many ups and downs. That's why this isn't really any kind of abyss, but sort of a people's pit, a communal lot, an histori-cal cache overflowing with the vapours of human warmth.

And what's in Kyiv? Indifference? Does no one want to know any-one? The internal pulling and tugging of tiny milieus inside their min-iature fortresses?

6

I don't like Kyiv – I wrote over two years ago. Back then I had a partic-ular reason for this – this city savagely murdered my friend. Honestly, this could have happened somewhere else, in any other city, in a differ-ent country, maybe even on another planet. But, at the same time, this was so Kyiv-like, this murder, this insanity, this death for nothing!

That's right, for nothing. In Kyiv you always sense this Nothing – from the human stream it flawlessly singles out all others, all those that are different, it closely follows their gesticulations, it monitors their lan-guage, it notices the stirring in their souls, and their most delicate mood swings. It's not necessarily about ruining those others – it's probably about (if I am capable of understanding such things) neutralizing, or perhaps, taming them. It evaluates them and doesn't let them out of its sight until their last breath. If we're going to mention an abyss, well this is it.

That morning I had just arrived in Kyiv and had lots that I wanted and didn't want to take care of, setting off as early as 8 a.m. to allow enough time to settle at least half of my promises and meets and greets. Around nine o'clock I was met with horrible news and I continued on, propelled just by inertia, because after news like that, everyday bus-tling about quickly loses any sense. But I was still able to cover those insane Kyiv distances – maybe this was an attempt at self-preservation or the illusion of escape. One way or another – I popped up from under-ground in many places, which, as a rule, were far away from each other. And everywhere I saw the same thing: meat sold from city stands. It was some kind of Meat Day all over Kyiv – by metro stations, improvised markets, on stairs, in squares and in courtyards some people sold meat from tables that were tacked with white tin and looked like morgue trolleys, butchering chunks, cracking bones, poplar fuzz, bees and flies circled around them, it was June, it was sticky and humid, the deathly Kyiv dust covered the stands, the animal carcasses, the face of the sell-ers and buyers, and they all continued to diligently and symmetrically do their job – they quartered, they weighed, they sniffed, they priced.

I guess this was some kind of humour. In this way, Nothing was making jokes. This was like a film brought on by the death of my friend. Nothing achieved its goal when about a week later a phrase was written, almost as if by itself: "I don't like Kyiv."

7

Nonetheless I need to go there – it's unavoidable, it is, as I wrote, a substantial part of my life, the road from Ivano-Frankivsk to Kyiv with a requisite stop in Lviv.

That time was pretty much the same, except that a major drop in temperature could already be felt on the Lviv train platform, so I couldn't leisurely enjoy my cigarette in the company of some distant acquaintances from the neighbouring train car. I lay down to sleep almost right away because I knew they'd be waking me up at 5 a.m. – the train car needed to be tidied up before it arrived in Kyiv. In fact, the train attendant didn't even give me a chance to lie down much and growled, in Russian, "mushchina padiom!" (yo guy, up and at 'em!) in my ear. The hands of my watch were illuminated in the dark. It was quarter to five. Clenching my teeth and cursing this most awful of worlds, I emerged from under my overcoat into the cold. It was extremely difficult to clean the train vestibule from the endless array of cigarette butts stuck frozen to the slippery floor, covered with bloody clumps. I recalled that around 1 a.m. I heard the noise of a fight emanating from the vestibule of the train. A most unfortunate development, I thought to myself. The shitter required about five buckets of ice-cold water. During all of this, other passengers – women with down kerchiefs and loud veterans with military ribbons – got in my way. I finished washing the corridor in a panic, just as the train began braking at the Kyiv train station.

Kyiv was dark, and I used my instincts to find the path into the train station. As I walked, taxi drivers got in my way, they grabbed at my elbows and at the edges of my coat, flashing cigarette lighters in my face. Though they may not have been taxi drivers. Breaking through their perimeter I managed to get to the waiting room, but there were so many reeking bums, cripples, gypsies, and wackos, that I was forced to turn around right at the entrance upon seeing a thuggish-looking cop, who was walking right at me.

I remembered that I had a very busy day ahead of me in Kyiv: a live TV appearance, an appointment with the publishing board of directors, for which I hadn't had time to look over the necessary paperwork, a crucial meeting, in English or German, with the Dutch attaché, a coordinating committee with all of its internal intrigue, my solo performance in the Teachers Building, and that which lies underneath. Taking all of this into account, I had to clean myself up somehow after that horrible train ride. This could only be taken care of in the public restroom, but that huge, glowing letter "M," towards which I gravitated, turned out to be the entrance to the metro. The line for metro tokens moved so slowly that I had time to notice the pregnant women in line fainting, how pickpockets got to work (there were about ten of them, and one of them flashed me his knife, when our glances met by chance), and then, finally, how an enraged ticket agent poked an annoying client in the eye with a pencil. The latter clutched his face, his eye dripping through his fingers. I sensed that I knew that guy. I think we had travelled on the same train.

Riding on the escalator I soon understood that I had come too early – raids usually take place in the Kyiv metro during these morning hours. And they do indeed – the bottom of the escalator was policed by a couple of thugs in army-issue coats. They had already captured a pair of poor souls for army service. I began frantically trying to remember which years I had actually served in the army, so I could at least tell them something, but this, people say, doesn't help much. There was only one way out – turn around and run up the escalator stairs, which were moving downward. I saw people do this in films, so I figured that it might be a realistic option.

Here's what wasn't realistic: to make it past this darkness, through these people with their bodies and clothes, through crutches, mangled hands, gold teeth, palms wide open, gaping mouths, through sacks full of chewy meat, through the stiff, cold air. At that moment I decided that never again would I come to Kyiv, sensing with horror that it's too late for such promises.

"Wake up, passengers, we arrive in Kyiv in an hour," the train attendant said not really all that angrily. I returned to my own body as if back into my coupé. It was completely light outside, the clock showed 5:30 a.m.

The best part of horrible dreams is when they end. You know about this, Kyiv.

1999

What Language Are You From: A Ukrainian Writer among the Temptations of Temporariness

TRANSLATED BY MARK ANDRYCZYK

An excerpt from a lecture read at Cambridge University during the annual conference of the British Association for Slavonic and East European Studies (BASEES) on 7 April 2002.

1

The idea for this presentation came to me from two main premises, on which I will attempt to rely as much as my very irregular system of beliefs will allow. Actually, it is not so much a *system* and not *beliefs*, but a list of chaotic assumptions that, for some reason, here and now, still seem to have certain merit. Thus, I must ask you to indulge me. And if I can use this as some kind of justification, then I humbly ask that you take into consideration that all my forthcoming statements are, in one way or another, borrowed, and usually overheard. I like to listen to the conversations of people who are much more well-read than I am and try to catch something from them for myself – this is one way of saving yourself from having to read and mull over original sources, in other words, a way to save time. And time was and remains one of my chief heroes of being.

So, my first premise is based on the idea that the existence of language, and, consequently, languages, is most probably transitory. There is no need to dwell for a long time on the idea that languages, like human individuals, their carriers, have a tendency to be born and to die, together with all – in some cases more evident, in others less so – apparent intermediate stages: establishment, flowering, decline, and all those that follow. After all, the existence of a language as a means – let's call it a *means of communication* – is also, obviously, transitory, which allows a Ukrainian writer-colleague of mine ready to claim that the existence of language is rudimentary. But I would not go that far and will instead limit myself to the issues that pertain not to language in general, but to its concrete manifestations – languages.

So then – returning to the idea of their transitoriness. Literary texts in any language are mainly born as a protest against this transitoriness. Even people who write are not often conscious of this motive for writing. But that's exactly how it is: every phenomenon of literary creation is a manifestation of the battle of language for itself, its – most often, desperate – self-defence. Thus, for every language, a literary text is an opportunity to prolong its existence as much as possible. From that point of view, writers are tools of sorts, through which this despair of transitoriness speaks, but if you find that judgment to be too metaphysical, then let's simply call them doers or, perhaps more aptly – agents.

And here we can, painstakingly and at length, try to find the second, genitive, part of the metaphor – agents of what? The most histrionic among us would say – agents of eternity. But what can we know about eternity except that an inhuman chill gusts from it? Someone with more restraint in their feelings and expressions would say – agents of continuity. But we really can't imagine the development of language and then literature as a succession, all tidily and neatly wrapped in time. And someone else may say – agents of durability. But that could only be said in bitter jest: how can one speak of durability when the building materials of this, shall we say, structure, are the most ephemeral ones of all – nothing but words, words, words?

I would call writers agents of a universal emergency rescue squad. Its work involves many traces of manipulation, phoniness, bustling external stimulation, a panicky battle for each exhale and each inhale. The power of writers' ability (solely indigenous to them) to realize themselves exceptionally through certain words of a certain language – unknowingly, I surmise – gives that language a chance to exist a bit longer. And this is first and foremost the case with languages, which have been teetering at the border of existence and disappearance for decades, if not centuries. Like Ukrainian, for example.

My second premise is the idea that a writer is involved in the vanity of vanities. And it is within this uselessness that a writer has to feel like a fish in water, in this fleeting, transitory concrete thing, in the conjuncture of this concrete thing. The sharper a writer's attention to transitoriness, to all its finest details, to shades and insinuations, passing blackouts, subjective glows, clever architectural ensembles, changeable landscapes, movable menageries, to city plans, maps, traffic patterns and postcards, to hotel rooms, cigarette brands, types of alcohol, scents, tastes and aftertastes, as well as to thousands of manifestations of solely physiological memory, in other words, the sharper a writer's attention to *a madeleine*, the better the chance for transitoriness overcoming its own boundaries. Exactly in such a manner – because it's not about eternity, which as we've agreed, we are better off without – it is about overcoming the boundaries of transitoriness.

In light of such a nature, more precisely, dependence, a writer can perhaps be seen as the type of person most easily prone to temptation. Anyone who has learned how to raise themselves above temptations has no need to write, they are silent (and if they do write, they write criminally badly) – and they don't concern us here. Writing is the concentrated temptation of everything else: power, knowledge, taking control, sex, a parallel reality. Thus, it is within a writer's writing that all the mentioned and unmentioned demons coordinate and concentrate their strengths. That is why writing as such is, in fact, the ultimate temptation.

Today I would like to deliberate a bit, out loud, about the way that this ultimate temptation reveals itself for a Ukrainian writer, that is, for a writer who writes in Ukrainian. Thus, I will primarily try to determine something regarding the temptations to write in the Ukrainian language. This temptation only recently reached its two-hundredth year – a period of time that belongs to a category that is usually termed *pitifully short*.

2

1798 – the year of the robust rotting away of the Baroque and straining post-enlightenment Classicism – provided future Ukraine with the beginning of its literature in the form of an unsanctioned-by-the-author, and thus, pirated, publication of the first three parts of the mock epic *Eneida* by Ivan Kotliarevsky – an extremely inventive and joyful work. The humorous nature of *Eneida* lies primarily in the combination of the un-combinable, that is, in bringing together in a very witty pastiche two universes that are far from each other – Virgil's heroic epic of antiquity *The Aeneid* and comically parodic, emphatically profane Cossack-seminary-student's poetic versification. Literary historians have long ago concurred about the travesty-burlesque character of this first epic poem written in Ukrainian vernacular.

The author of *Eneida* was a representative of the *middle-class* of that time, a provincial public servant and retired officer, Ivan Kotliarevsky, a guy with sufficient refinement to tastefully lampoon his own era. To understand the true sense of this lampooning one must first discern the taste of intellectual revenge. This was a fully colonized culture mocking imperial culture, its colonizer. And mocking itself as well – that is why we notice in *Eneida* a completely egregious, in the Classicistic context of that time, ethical and aesthetic ambivalence.

Kotliarevsky as a person requires a bit more attention. Two hundred years ago, this unusually happy twenty-nine-year-old travelling teacher, who educated the children of noblemen and had a sound knowledge of cooking, alcohol, maps, and cards, unexpectedly to himself became the author of the world's first truly Ukrainian book. For the following forty years of his life, he was involved with many important and not so important things – he tried to get married, served in the army, fought against Napoleon, and wrote new parts of *Eneida*, gradually developing a belief in the seriousness of this game and in the inevitability of this mission; later, he led a theatre, assembling the first national vaudevilles for it, he scribbled various *odes to princes*, collected culinary recipes, having delved, for the last two decades of his life, into mysticism and having become interested in para-Christian symbols, worked on a translation of the Gospels, or at least all kinds of French *supplements to the Gospels*. If one takes genius to be something in between misunderstanding and coincidence, then that is what we have here, genius.

Of course, you can look for the actual beginning of literature in many different places. Constructing the myth of the First Book, the Cosmos-Book, the national Book of Genesis, one can turn to Veles and Nestor, to Monomakh and Boyan, to, say, Illarion or to the for-better-or-worse Irish monk Riangabar, who defended medieval Kyiv from the Mongols, one can turn to countless other tales, testaments, laments, and legends, one can project this deeper and deeper, to, for example, some sort of Sumerian-Akkado-Indoaryan foundations and proto-sources; one can, in fact, create one's own clever falsifications to no end – enough parallels, similarities, epiphanies, and comparative-etymological allusions can be found.

But this is precisely the origin I like, the Kotliarevsky one. I like the fact that Ukrainian literature began almost in jest – simply as a game for a tiny circle of close friends and Monday guests, who would gather in Kotliarevsky's Poltava home at exceptionally bountiful, arranged dinners (a repeated list of the various dishes and drinks served are provided throughout *Eneida* itself). At some point, obviously, between the tasting of spirits, the smoking of cigars, and a round of Boston or Whist, opportunities emerged to read the poem's latest fragments out loud. *Eneida* was written on a "to be continued ..." basis – from one reception to the other, from one public opportunity to another. This was a project stretched out over a rather long period of time – Kotliarevsky worked on it for a drawn-out twenty-six years, in other words, not much less time than Goethe spent on his *Faust* – if such a comparison does not look too much like blasphemy.

I enjoy the fact that the author of these versified provocations was admired in his circles, that his vulgarisms gave birth to a multi-year fad of all things Ukrainian in the higher echelons of society, that he received enough sinecure from the powers that be and that he didn't need to consider his creative work to be a self-sacrifice. I like the fact that this creative work was not coerced. In other words, it was free.

In addition, I like the fact that akin to, for example, Mozart, Kotliarevsky was a mason and belonged to the "Love for Truth" lodge, and thus was part to the Astreia union. Kotliarevsky's secret position in the lodge had the title *vitiia* – thus, once again, we have a reference to the weaving from words of an extraordinary, unfamiliar to any previously existing, fabric. A system of secret signs, an exchange of rings, esoteric card games, and cultish musical parties – all of these attributes perfectly fit his brilliantly layered soul. By the way, I can't wait for school research papers to be written on the topic "Ukrainian Literature as the Birth of the Worldwide Masonic Conspiracy."

And finally, I like the fact that it, this literature, began with a pirated bestseller. That its large publishing runs consistently sold well – this forced the author, as he was finishing writing the epic poem's next part, including the chapter about Enei's journey through hell, to curse the pirate-publisher with eternal anguish. At the margins of history – well, of this story, at least – we have two emperors – the Russian Alexander and the French Napoleon. The former presented Kotliarevsky with a diamond ring, a major's rank, and a pension. The latter, while escaping from Moscow, picked up a copy of the *Eneida* – perhaps as a good luck charm or as what he thought to be a holy text written in esoteric letters. All of this cannot but enchant: it's a good thing that the beginning of literature in the language, that today is regarded as Ukrainian, was just as it was – pleasurable, playful, and pirated.

3

Two hundred years after Kotliarevsky's brazen appeal, the temptation to write in Ukrainian remains just as sweet. We should be thankful to the

Russian Empire in all of its historical manifestations, the Soviet Union included, for this. The history of Ukrainian literature within the borders of this empire is a history of prohibitions and restrictions. I am not at all trying to exaggerate when I venture to say that this is a history of censorship and, in parallel, of samizdat. The ghost of *Ukrainian separatism and self-defining movements* invariably appeared where, even without it, the atmosphere of intellectual life already swelled with constant suspicions and denunciations. Between the prohibiting circulars issued by the Russian ministers of police, contemporaries of Maeterlinck and Rimbaud, and the complete annihilation of the entire Ukrainian literary scene in the early 1930s by the Chekists,[1] contemporaries of Rolland and Gide, lies not just a slice of time a half-a-century thick, but an entire abyss beyond time of exhaustingly dramatic resistance between the system and an individual. The system won, of course. In the sense that language, deprived of a self-sufficiently free existence, could not realize itself in a self-sufficiently free literary text. That is, taking into account my premise today, language was incapable of overcoming the boundaries of its own transitoriness – it, fully and completely, belonged to this transitoriness, when it was intensely concerned only with its own survival and nothing else.

Poetry is a form of survival for a language. The last of the *great Ukrainian poets* (I employ the very special, traditionally messianic connotations of this concept), Vasyl Stus, was destroyed in a Soviet prison camp in the not-so-distant year of 1985, during the time of the not-so-cruel, and not-so-rigid rule of General Secretary Gorbachev.

But all these prophylactic imperial measures paradoxically resulted in a situation in which the Ukrainian language could not get tired and old. That is, today, as it was two hundred years ago, situated on the curiously favourable edge of balancing between rebirth and degeneration, it maintains those characteristics that are perhaps most tempting for a writer: yet to be fully formed, vacant, ambivalent, flexible and, most importantly – omnipotent, or as my colleague Taras Prokhasko says – totipotent, all-capable.

This gives me grounds to presume that it, language, had a giddy youth. On the highest level it remains wide open for anything and, if you allow me to share a clandestine truth, it is our writers today who are deciding the way this language will be perceived tomorrow.

4

Another major advantage, caused by empire and colonial–post-colonial status, that a Ukrainian writer's language has is that it is hidden from the world. No, not that it is closed off, but that it is hidden. What do I have in mind here?

Most of my Western colleagues begin with a belief that it does not exist at all or, at best, that it is something like a modified version of the Russian language, which has come about because of the political developments of the past decade. Taking this notion somewhat further, The Microsoft Encarta Encyclopedia, for example, tells us that "Ukrainian is the official language of Ukraine. It is also spoken in parts of nearby countries, such as Poland and the Czech Republic. *It is very similar to Russian*. Ukrainian uses the Cyrillic alphabet."

I pretend that I am a casual forager of information, based somewhere in some kind of Cambridge, United Kingdom, who, for some unknown reason is trying to use Microsoft to find out something about the word *Ukrainian*. But the complier of this – I must admit, rather user-friendly encyclopedia – basically offers only one characteristic: *It is very similar to Russian*. My casual forager of information will not stop there: he clicks on the link *Russian*, the definition of which will help him to understand what this Ukrainian is. And he reads that: "Russian is the official language of Russia. It is also spoken in a number of nearby countries. Written in the Cyrillic alphabet, which was developed from Greek. Russian is known for its many long words." Wonderful, says the forager of information (aka – the truth). Ukrainian is very similar to Russian. Russian is known for its very long words. Ergo, Ukrainian also has a lot of long words?

Perhaps that is indeed the case – I never tried to measure the average length of Ukrainian words on purpose. I'm concerned with something else here.

The Ukrainian language's state of being hidden – is the result of it being in the dense shadow of the Russian language – something that is much larger, more perceptible, better known, more powerful, and – correspondingly – immeasurably more actively present in the world's collective consciousness.

But why do I consider this state of being hidden, that is, this unquestionable obstacle on the path of the language being recognized and affirmed in the world, to be simultaneously an advantage?

I would answer this question in a more detailed manner, using such ephemerides as potential surprise, an information breakthrough, or cultural revolt. The state of being hidden can lead to an accumulation of quality, including literary quality. That quality, with its exploding inevitability, will emerge the moment we move out of the shadow. And in a very Dao-like manner: we will be noticed once we have matured for this, that is, come about, that is, finished, that is, died.

But I don't want to take up your attention with such theoretical things. In truth, a rather painful knot has become twisted by all this.

5

Not long ago, I watched a videotape of a film produced by a German television company on the ARTE channel. The film was about the "still unknown Europe" – about the western Ukrainian city of Lviv, about its foothills, about Carpathian sorcerers, about the "Centre of Europe," as the Emperor-King's geographers called it, and about other enticements of the world in which I live, from which I sometimes escape and to which I undoubtedly return after each escape. The film was very – what's the word – *cute* – probably just what tourists from "Europe #1" overflowing with canaries and majorcas need: lots of architecture, trees, picturesque ruins and cemeteries, unusual trolleys, the green colour of hope, lively street scenes, cafes, markets. I thought to myself that, if I hadn't already been living here since I was born, I would definitely like to visit this place.

But there was something in that film that would occasionally mar my generally good-natured countenance with a crooked grin, something disruptive. Well of course – it's those old women with kerchiefs on their heads again! The city was brimming with them – the obstinacy with which the camera would search for them over and over was almost maniacal. Old Ukrainian grandmas, portly and toothless, shabbily and carelessly dressed, with dull eyes, sometimes begging, but mostly – dying.

I protested internally because for me Lviv is a city that I always associated with, and will probably always associate with, youth. And I'm convinced that it is impossible that there are more old female faces in it than there are, for example, young female legs. Lviv is incredibly erotic, it is completely charged with flirting, dancing, exchanging glances. How could they not have noticed this?

But then I immediately calmed myself with the not very original thought that, when in a new country, we all see mostly what we set out to see. When I first visited America, I saw skyscrapers. The German cameramen who visited us knew that this is a country with a declining population and that old women a) live on twenty-five marks a month and b) wear kerchiefs on their heads. That is why their cameras so hypnotically turned towards the expected.

6

But, in general, the problem of the contemporary Ukrainian writer in his relationship with the external world does not stem from these partial stereotypes. Most of the time it stems from the fact that Western colleagues or, even more widely – the so-called *reading public* – doesn't really believe in the existence of that writer's language itself (well that's what you get for hiding in that comfortable Russian shadow!).

In the best-case scenario, they'll consider this language to be some type of version of Russian, which I've already talked about. Another, no less popular, concept – that it is just a falsely created and prescribed – especially over the past decade of the country's screwed-up independence – linguistic simulacrum, perhaps, useful for official functioning at the level of government documents. But true literature cannot be prescribed – its whole essence lies in it being breathed freely and not being forced. Ivan Kotliarevsky can attest to this.

And from this comes the greatest intrigue and most enamouring drama of the contemporary Ukrainian writer: the need to prove to the whole world, and, most importantly to himself, that the language that he writes in is in no way a creation of some new government officials and not a hazy hallucination of dreaming separatists. This recalls the need to, once and again, repeat out loud, in rather dignified, electrifying, and vociferous company, where, for some reason, nobody wants to notice you: I – am. And in such a situation it is quite difficult to be heard, without simultaneously slipping into a falsetto.

7

In all of this there is at least one rather uplifting conclusion: a province that moves past its own boundaries cannot help but entice. The Ukrainian province entices twofold, because it is a province of a province – the one that is called the Ukrainian metropolis. It is well known that the most interesting things take place at the margins, at the edges and environs, at painful stitches, at borderlands.

8

But all this is seen differently from the centres.

I recall an episode that occurred during one of the countless seminars that took place over the past decade – let's give it the conditional title "East-West." The seminar took place in a *conditionally transitional* zone, that is, in Vienna, and the topic, as always, was enticement, more specifically, how authors from Eastern Europe can successfully publish in the West. So, invited from the East were writers (as we've already agreed – agents of an emergency rescue squad) and from the West – simply agents and managers. The former mostly just listened, the latter formulated recommendations. You should focus more on love stories, they said. And less ornamentation – try to keep it to one hundred typed pages, max.

A certain lady from France advised her Eastern European colleagues that the most important thing they should do was change their first names and surnames. With those kinds of names don't even dream about any popularity, she warned us. They're impossible to read, let alone pronounce. Those awkward consonants, absurd sibilants, all those diacritical marks, and so on – all of this undeniably drives away your potential reader right from the book's cover. Your surnames should be easy and easily graspable – like, for example, *Kundera*.

Second, she went on, all of you need to master one of the world's major languages – preferably French – and to such an extent that all your future works will be written in that language. Exchanging a provincial language for one of the world's major languages is like going from the ghetto to a completely different space, one of much greater proportions than the previous one. You must admit that in this manner, other, not previously imagined perspectives will open up before you (and here she, for the second time, mentioned Mr *Kundera* – as if she were his agent, actually, she probably was).

There is also a "thirdly," an author jumped up from his seat, an inhabitant of an East European country that was either destroyed, or, conversely, created, during World War II. Changing one's name and language is far from all that needs to be done to obtain real success, he, for some reason, said agitatedly. You must also stop being yourself.

The woman from France, it seems, did not understand what he meant by this.

Well then – what? Stop being yourself? I suppose that's another potential way out. But will it be possible in such a case to maintain the sense of the message – when, bedeviled with helplessness and transitoriness, out of the transitory words of the only transitory language possible for you, you try to formulate your hopeless argument about something more long-lasting?

9

I have been bestowed with a surname that is especially long and difficult to read, which, on top of that, is written differently in every European language. I don't know any of the world's major languages well enough to live in it or, at least, to write a love story one hundred pages long. I can't cease being myself, regardless of how much I'd love to be different – brilliant, easygoing, cosmopolitan.

I live in a country which will not let me leave it for good – it has grabbed onto the lining of my coat with its spasmodic joints, ready to tear me to shreds with its great love. I have to reply in the same manner – to love this special warmth of vodka, this hazy light, these people, who don't want to believe a single one of my words and those, who toss away my words, to see how words start to lose any meaning at all, to delve ever deeper into pessimism, to love this comatose state, this sense of quagmire, from which there is no reason to leave, to love my final territory, in which, so far, it has been impossible to hunt me down. Thus, until it, my native country, triumphantly grabs me by the throat, I am in one way or another destined to utter my transitory words. All this love, to be honest, is a form of hate. And hate – a form of love. But you won't amaze any of us with this: everything is so very close.

I hide out in language as if in political asylum. It doesn't really look like a tower, and definitely not an ivory one – it's more like an unfinished, rickety shack, so it won't protect me, quite the opposite. All that I can extract in its defence consists of its own resources, and my task is to find them within it and, bit by bit, prolong its future. I surmise that if we have one another, we'll hang on for a bit longer.

I'm left with being myself and thinking about how to write better. There is no justification for this – eternity probably won't notice anything. Always and everywhere it comes down to the same thing: the adequacy of your efforts towards your enticements.

2002

Meeting Place Germaschka

TRANSLATED BY MARK ANDRYCZYK

Germany, of course, is a beautiful country.
Now if only there were no Germans there!
Thoughts expressed out loud, by a former compatriot of mine.

Berlin, 1994

1

It would be hard to prove that the climate of the country in which I was born and in which I live is very different from that in Middle Europe. It's the same – a summer that is usually cool in June and sweltering in August, the same variable winter with its temporary freezing temperatures and long thaws, the same autumn with the scent of rain and dying plants, the same nervous spring, filled with emotional anticipation. I bet that in the families of German veterans of the Eastern Front, all kinds of phantasmagoric and Münchhausen-like stories still circulate about Ukrainian winters, the world's harshest, which culminate with depictions of frostbitten extremities and frozen genitals. And this too is completely possible: the tendency of a person's memory to transform the real into the unreal and to accumulate narrational "special effects." I don't reject the idea that the climate can change and that the weather in Ukraine has indeed gotten less harsh since our lands last saw war. In any case, I can confirm with all the trustworthiness of a traveller that, over the last ten years, I've entered the Western world countless times and have returned the same amount of times: no, I don't see any climatic difference between Vienna and Lviv or Berlin and Kyiv.

However, on the other hand, that same inner traveller in me screams out his observations of a real, new Border. That Border traces the western national border of Ukraine, recreating, millimetre by millimetre, the former national border of the USSR, and, in this manner, dividing existence into Europe and Something Else. So then: over the past decade I have accumulated much experience in crossing this Border in both directions – there and back. And, in doing this, I used the forms of land transport that are traditional for these expanses and, someday, I'll write a whole book about all my encounters with border and customs officers. But not now. Now, I'm addressing an entirely strange phenomenon that accompanies it – The Border. Thus, notwithstanding the complete similarity of climates on both sides of it, when I cross it in the reverse direction, from West to East, I notice the same thing over and over: the weather suddenly getting worse, some kind of cataclysmic shift, a severe darkening of the landscape, the rankling of the heavens with rain or snow and, at best, perspectives filling with fog and greyness. It's as if each and every time, someone puts on a massive atmospheric show entitled "The Homeland Welcomes You!" especially for me, and my random fellow travellers. Or, at the threshold, they administer a test of my love for it: will he survive this time?

I don't doubt that the problem here is with me. But I generally do love returning very much, and you can't scare me with these kinds of cataclysms.

2

And what exactly does this fatal, post-Soviet Border disconnect from Europe? In other words, what need is there for the radiant European Union, while it continually grows eastward, to separate itself from these *pallid abandoned territories* with a new iron curtain? Could it once again be about disconnecting the light from the dark? But then why is this light in the West? And why is the darkness in the East? Maybe it's because of our energy problems, because of the consistent blackouts in the fall-winter season, because of how, every evening, our cities, towns, and villages fall into the jaws of night?

So what separates us? Well, for starters, it obviously has to be – the different quality of our roads. Having crossed The Border and set upon the *bosom of the fatherland*, I begin to physically feel this horribly deteriorated, furrowed with cracks, resurfaced a thousand times but left for destruction, surface. I'm shaken and tossed about, and the driver cannot go any faster than sixty kilometres an hour or so, and every pothole very expressively shows an obvious lack of belonging to Greco-Roman civilization. But even if you avoid roadways for automobiles and turn to the mercy of the railways – The Border will nonetheless differentiate *European* railroad tracks from those of a *Russian* width. And what do you do with those railroad tracks, this, perhaps, most indigestible inheritance from the empire?

Actually, no. It's not the tracks, more specifically not their augmented width, that best demonstrates a true, uninterrupted imperial existence but, instead, different music and a different mass culture in general. It is The Border that separates lands where Russian pop music is listened to with great enthusiasm from those lands where it is disparaged. It's truly amazing: just two or three kilometres to the West and it turns out that no one here has even heard of Fillip Kirkorov or Alla Pugacheva, or, moreover, of Iosif Kobzon, that Frank Sinatra of the still-united post-Soviet space. But just two to three kilometres East and the abovementioned Fillip, Alla, and Iosif grow to legends of titanic proportions among the folk, they are like favourite family members and are much more cherished and better understood than all, without exception, national-state ideals and successes, including Ukraine's European choice. I have no doubt that the USSR continues to exist – as a gigantic and indivisible slab of dry land, *one sixth of the Earth's surface*, where it is customary to love bad Russian music (no, not Tchaikovsky and not Mussorgsky – they are listened to farther to the West).

And from there – and tied to that kind of music is the cog of life, this entire daily ritual with different rules for relationships, with a different – collective – ethic, with different concepts of friendship, and also with different drinks, both at celebrations and every day. The vodka zone, although it begins farther West, in the neighbouring and in many ways positive example that is Poland, here, on this side of The Border, takes on its most complete manifestation – because the official price of vodka here is so much lower than in Poland that it instantly transforms from being an emblematic element of entertainment to being daily bread and something that is as unavoidable as air.

And this difference cannot help but be exemplified in people's clothing as well. Yes, The Border also differentiates manners of dress – there they are, those winter hats made of rabbit fur, those down kerchiefs on the heads of older women, those heavy and formless things, fully oriented towards the cold seasons of the year (and, in this manner, creating a mirror-like reflection of the abovementioned myth about Ukraine having the harshest winters, paradoxically adapted from those very same veterans of the Wehrmacht), and also that prevalence of baggy sweat suits and all kinds of fake leather. And even the boundless piles of cheap *European* second-hand clothes, which have blossomed over the past five years at our, also boundless, markets, have been unable to markedly induce a pro-Western change in the outlines of the people's landscape.

Because this landscape is determined, first and foremost, by something that is more important than the political system of the past hundred or two hundred years or even more important than the Cyrillic alphabet, which is so exotically pleasant to the eye of the truly refined European person who, in order to establish his own personal linguistic uniqueness, has to settle for the meagre options offered by diacritical marks and explain his own historical-cultural exceptionality to a certain, let's say, *eszett*.[1] But no – that's not it, it's not the beauty of the Cyrillic alphabet in its Ukrainian version, not *the crescent moon of the letter* є or *the thin little candle of the letter* ї, that makes what is on the other side of The Border different.

No, this difference has within it something deeper and more basic – maybe it's a Byzantine mentality, according to which *truth is greater than the law*. And because, simultaneously, *to each his own truth*, any Western attempt to instill on the other side of The Border its *rule of law* is destined to get booed and sabotaged. The most far-sighted of sociopsychologists have long ago provided their diagnosis that absolute despotism is the only possible form of at least some kind of rule over such a Byzantinized society and that no democratic models will work here because they transform into some kind of completely monstrous post-totalitarian metamorphoses, or, perhaps more accurately, metastases.

But I don't want to come to terms with this – honestly, I like near-sightedness much better than far-sightedness and therefore, I don't want to give up my final territories to some absolute despotism.

Instead, I completely agree that in the final division of the world one can talk about the difference in people's faces. It's like a riddle: why do I always and everywhere recognize those faces from my side of The Border? Why is it so, regardless of where I see them, whether in the Vienna Opera or in a Venetian hostel, independent of their surrounding entourage and clothing? And taking into account all genetic variations and typological erosions – why?

3

Those faces (Ukrainian? Post-Soviet? Soviet Ukrainian?) are more and more prevalent in the West. With every visit there I notice again and again there are more of them. In bureacratic slang this is known as *vyizd na PeEmZhe*. The use of abbreviations, that indigestible sociolinguistic sign of a Soviet person, has been successfully maintained in a post-Soviet one. Which, in my view, only confirms the clandestine notion that homo post-sovieticus is really just a division of the homo sovieticus, just some type of historical branching off. I could go even further and widen this notion to the level of the whole system: the USSR actually continues to exist – having been denied its external face, it unyieldingly maintains its internal – inside, it continues to cover its most spacious one-sixth surface of the brain's hemisphere on the subcortical level, in nerve cells that, by the way, regenerate regardless of being informed of their complete inability to regenerate. Well then: these do regenerate.

But let's return to the already mentioned *vyizd na PeEmZhe*. This abbreviation, which was created, without a doubt, in the tangled labyrinth Soviet/post-Soviet police offices of visas and registration, is made up of three Russian words: *postoiannoe mesto zhytel'stva* (permanent place of residence). It's understood that here we have the historical echo of serfdom, characteristic of tsarist Russia and, moreover, the bureaucratic police notion of disallowed or, at least, undesired displacement of any individual without control from the top.

In everyday language, *vyizd na PeEmZhe* (leaving for your permanent place of residence) could be phrased as, let's say – leaving for good. That is, information stating that Mr X *vyizhdzhaie na PeEmZhe v eferge* (is leaving for PeEmZhe to FRG) should be understood to be that Mr X has obtained permission for permanent residency in Germany and that he now couldn't give a rat's ass about anything to do with Ukraine and that he's leaving it as soon as he can so he can end up on the other side of the Border as soon as he can, to become a *normal person* and, if possible, never cross back over The Border.

In the more noble past (and, for some reason, the past always seems more noble than the present), when dealing with ideological wars against a system, *vyizd na PeEmZhe* was called *emigration*. These were odd individuals – those who were brave enough to emigrate: brainy dissident professors, writers, artists and directors of theatres, political prisoners who were released because of the efforts of Amnesty International.

This had to be the courage that Camus once wrote about – the courage of a deserter in a time of war. Using moral blackmail rather well, the system manipulated the stereotypes of desertion and betrayal: every emigrant, in one way or another, was publicly and loudly branded and consigned to slander by the community. This required an absolute ability to burn bridges behind you – to be able to sidestep all branding and slander. The people of the emigration were usually a rather stubborn and self-assured version of the *antisovieticus*. Their choice was, without a doubt, an extreme choice, it required an otherness, a different way of thinking and feeling.

The *PeEmZhe* type of person today is entirely mutable. He longs not for the distinctive but for the typical. He usually is indeed that very same homo sovieticus, who could not find a place for himself among the fragments of a seemingly collapsed system. The already-ephemeral notion of "fatherland" lost all sense for him and now, completed disoriented, he set out for those lands that have the best-stocked stores. I will permit myself to call these people the *Woolworth people*. I do this completely conditionally. Instead of Woolworth it could be Aldi or something of that nature. The meaning is the same: these are people who broke through The Border with a subconscious longing for that socialism that was lost on the other side of The Border. Woolworth supermarkets are a completely socialist model of equalized welfare – with a limited selection and the comparatively low-level quality of its goods but – and this is most important – with low prices and with a, let's say, rather egalitarian form of presentation.

Socialism is when you are cared for from the top. This is social aid (in the slang of PeEmZhe people – *sotsial*), on which you can successfully live in a new place of residence, a Germacshka filled with the blessings of *Vulvort*. Used to a lack of consumer goods for several generations, the *PeEmZhe people* basically don't need anything else: the goal has been reached, heaven on earth has been achieved and, as they often joke in their circle, *zhyzn' udalasia* (in Russian – life was a success).

I recall a story I saw on a certain German television channel ten years ago, when I visited territories on the other side of The Border for the first time. There was a shot of, in the words of the commentator, a *refugee from Ukraine* – a young man, no older than thirty; he made contorted, anguished faces and, with a quivering voice, said that he escaped a place where, after the fall of the USSR, total catastrophe reigns, with the threat of civil war; this was all said in Russian and, for some reason, the synchronic translation that was provided off screen greatly exaggerated the report of apocalyptic life described by the man; the viewer must have imagined a true, postwar landscape with human bodies, unburied and shredded by crazed dogs close up; at the conclusion, the guy stated that he had already begun learning German and that he is incredibly thankful to the *German government,* etc., because the place from where he had escaped was – *kein Lebensmittel.*[2] It seems that this was one of the first German words he had learned – *Lebensmittel,* because he managed to repeat it about ten times, it was like an invocation (hier viel Lebensmittel, dort kein Lebensmittel), this was the highest form of invocation – prayer, it was like a Woolworth-mantra – yes indeed, because it was about religion, about the special religion of the Soviet people and about their supreme deities, which have the name, for example, Lebensmittel.

4

Figuratively speaking, the countries of the world can be divided into those from which people escape, and those to which people escape. Germany, without a doubt, belongs to the latter, which in itself should increase its citizens' sense of pride. Obviously, this division that I have proposed screams of its incorrectness because what then are we to do, for example, with Poland, to which Ukrainians and Romanians escape en masse, but from where, at the same time, Polish labour migrants escape to this day? No, this world does not give in to generalities and schematics, it does not fit within the frames of the aforementioned, *figuratively speaking* – and this is good!

But let's leave Poland alone with its definitively outlined aspirations to the European Union and all of its very high standards. I live in a country, which one could *figuratively* place among those countries of the first type. People escape from it. Both temporarily and for good.

Ukrainians migrate, and the grounds exist to say that they migrate en masse. There are no official statistics because 90 per cent of this migration is illegal. According to one particular unofficial statistic, in Portugal itself there are almost three hundred thousand, with about the same amount in Greece and, in Italy, there are almost one million. Ukrainians migrate and mimic – in the face of the danger of police arrests, raids, and deportations. Even though there is a great risk of ending up in slavery, in a prison, or in a bordello, Ukrainians migrate nonetheless.

A few days ago I saw a translation of material that had just been published in the British journal *The Economist,* in which, perhaps for the first time in its ten-year history of independence, our country was described as being pitiful. No, I'm not trying to take anything out of context – the analyst of *The Economist* was generally full of positive intentions, he was not concerned with insults or complexes, he wrote that the West "would prefer to see Ukraine as a less frayed and pitiful neighbor of the European Union when neighbors of Ukraine, such as Poland and Hungary, are joining this western club."

But the word has been uttered: pitiful. And I can't do anything about it. Except, perhaps, to try and find a fable on a similar theme. Well here's one.

My friend, twelve years younger than me, lives in Prague. He comes from the Ukrainian National Republic emigration of 1920 and belongs to the third generation of that wave – not just he, but his father, too, were born in Czechoslovakia. Like all descendants of *political emigrants*, my friend undergoes a difficult evolution in self-identification: who is he? It turns out that this is still important even in today's not-yet-fully globalized world. On the one hand, he is torn by temptations of assimilation – become a *normal* Czech, go beyond the boundaries of the family-ancestral ghetto. On the other hand, stay true to that ancestry, together with its ghetto, and the temptations to preserve his Ukraini-anness intact. On top of that, my friend is a poet, thus, his choice in self-identification is not just a trivial matter: it comes down to choosing which language you will use to tell the world you are in love.

My friend really likes women (I shake his hand from afar) and falls in love very often. Almost every one of his new sweethearts, upon meeting him, asks him why he has such a strange name – Taras.[3] Since the mid-1990s my friend stopped giving his new sweethearts a truthful answer to their innocent question. And he has his own reasons for this. That is why none of the new girlfriends of my Prague friend know anything about his Ukrainian background and the unfamiliarity of his name, in their consciousness, probably straddles the realm of the exotic and the peculiar.

One time, a girl, whom he had considered to be the closest in the world for about a week already, arrived very late for a rendezvous. She explained her tardiness by saying that as soon as she left her home, a car sped by her and splashed her head to toe with rainwater. The girl had to go back home and change clothes because she could not be seen in public in such a horrible state! "Can you imagine," she found a comparison to better express herself, "I looked as filthy as a Ukrainian!" For my friend, who had been blessed with that great name, this became an intimate catastrophe. Not much later he stopped seeing the girl.

5

As is the case with millions of other people, I really like Prague, that quintessence of all possible mysteries and fantasies, the tangling of secrets, loves, the alchemy of grand and subtle gestures, it is, indeed, one of the few places on the map of the World's Theatre where the real and the surreal, the physical and the metaphysical, create a rather over-zealous indivisible whole.

But it turns out that there exists another Prague. I would sometimes chance upon it when I ran into some poorly dressed and drunken people in Prague's alleyways at night. This is the Prague of the Ukrainian migrant workers, the city into which tens (hundreds?) of thousands of my fellow countrymen have legally and illegally flowed. A city in which they get the most difficult and the dirtiest work for a laughably paltry wage. A city in which they agonize and get drunk, sleep in shacks and huts, and get caught for petty theft at markets. A city in which they are not liked, in which every one of them can simply get beaten up like a nasty dog by some middleman mafia guy. This is usually an underground world. Somewhere inside it, below the feet of tourists from all corners of the world, ten to twelve hours a day, citizens of Ukraine clean a hundred years of garbage out of medieval cellars. The aforementioned Prague girl was right about them: pushed beyond the bounds of the human and the humane, they truly are filthy. There's nothing new here: what we have is just the latest influx of the proletariat into Europe, and perhaps the blame for all this should fall on wild capitalism paired with Marx.

For me, on the other hand, for a person who is still trying to write there, in that place from where people are fleeing, this became just the latest collapse of a chronic, sickness-like, illusion.

6

The right to illusion probably belongs to the most fundamental of human rights. Objectively speaking – and here the run-of-the-mill, homegrown metaphysicist in me speaks – illusion lies somewhere in those spheres that are adjacent to hope. My personal illusion, which has been torn and battered many times, nonetheless still exists for me to this day, perhaps because it is mostly tied to a look to the West – there, into the evening twilight, above The Border. "Europe is …" – I try to designate with words the dizziness that has accumulated in me under the influence of illusion, – and, of course, again and again I keep on making the same grave mistakes.

It's been exactly ten years since I first ended up in my "Europe is . . ." Thus, my illusion was ten years bigger and younger, leading to lines being written on their own, which I read over today with a mix of shame and delight. For example:

> The European person was created by inheritance. You enter the world surrounded by towers and orchards, which are hundreds of years old. You are already too weak to cause any damage here – even if you really wanted to. Although this architecture is taken from the landscape, all of its creators are known by name. This victory over the most trivial, these coordinates of stability and transition themselves signify certain absolute values, among them – human individuality, separate, one and unrepeatable.

Oh what hymns to Europe I would sing ten years ago! Do I have any excuses at all for them?

First, I was charmed by the landscape. Ten years ago, having found myself in the West for the first time in that life I could not rid myself of the sense that all of this was a different planet. I read, guessed, and dreamed about it a lot, I fostered it inside me, completely illusionary, but all of my illusions turned out to be components of reality – that is why! It was the second month of our Ukrainian independence, it was January and there was no snow, a *young country* lay in dirt and in the dark, electricity was shut off from six to 9 p.m., candles and matches were becoming much more expensive, money inflated at a geometric-Homeric pace, and it was advantageous to spend it as soon as possible, well at least drink it away, but for some reason vodka was purchased with tickets, so – extremely long lines, the cold of unheated apartments, interruptions in the water supply, well then, of course – that son of a bitch on TV was right! – *kein Lebensmittel*.

And then, after a two-hour flight you, greenhorn and gawker, end up in a world where everything is different: an ancient villa, a park on the slope, chandeliers and mirrors, Secession-era stoves, cherrywood furniture, the steady functioning of mechanisms, the perfection of locks and switches, a focused silence, hot water, warmed wine and, most importantly – the Alps that are visible from the window. And also – the dizzying possibility of journeys and experiences, the freedom of movement, train stations, autobahns, mountain passes, thousand-year-old fortification walls, towers – everything I could fit in my convulsed

"Europe is . . ." And how can you then not become convinced by ideas such as "the European person was created by mountains and forests" and "existence must strive toward discretion, diversity and formal perfection?"

This was akin to love, I will add as an excuse. No, not akin to – it *was* love!

But who can tell me why today, exactly ten years later, when I once again received the same invitation to that park on the slope, why everything had become blurry and murky in my eyes? Where did this idiocy of suburban vacant lots and garbage dumps come from? Where did this Sovietization of space and breaking down of clocks come from? Why is it that Germany looks more and more like Germaschka? Why has it become so much more Eastern in ten years' time? No, not even more Eastern: having lost its Western polish, it didn't acquire an Eastern warmth. Well, where did it end up then? Is this just my illusion getting smaller and older over ten years' time? Did the Ukrainian landscape progress so much in those ten years that the German one no longer enchants me? It's hard to believe.

I surmise that the Woolworth people are in a large part responsible for all this erosion and tarnishing. This always happens when the only goal is simply to take.

7

The bus in which I travelled from Lviv to Munich on 2 November 2001 had close to seventy passengers – there were no empty seats. The bus in which I returned from Munich to Lviv on 30 January 2002 had seven passengers, just about ten times less. Perhaps this was a coincidence, or perhaps it was a tendency. Most probably, the latter: this is a place that people go to and don't return.

Nobody has the right to forbid others the search for a better life, not even a writer. Migration, that is *vyizd na PeEmZhe*, is such a search for a better life, no doubt about it. Then why do all these people irritate me so? Where does this almost passion come from – to not allow them to go there, through *PeEmZhe,* to my "Europe is …"? To all those parks on hills, to arches and towers, to thousand-year-old trees and fortification walls, and, most importantly, to Alpine ridges on the horizon outside the window? Because all of this is just my personal illusion, well-worn and refuted many times, it remains on its own, somewhere in me, inside, because Europe is really just a socialist Woolworth of sorts, where everyone is allowed to take without giving anything back in return.

So that probably is the issue: I am not bothered by the fact that they are looking for a better life, but by the idea that a better life for them is fully realized within the dimensions of a Woolworth. What bothers me is that they want so pitifully little from the world: social support. That, from existence, they are hoping for a used Audi or a Bimmer.[4] That, from Germany, they need Germaschka.

I sit next to them on the bus, like some absurd spy, who unintentionally is forced to listen to their conversations and who looks suspicious, for starters, because of his isolated incommunicability. He seems to be not one of us. Maybe he was sent by the Polish border control. Interpol? Abwehr?[5]

The bus is an exterritorial thing, that is, in it, they act as though they are at home. I don't want to say anything bad: they nonetheless remain collectivists, sharing food, drinks, and cigarettes, watching, with amazement, Russian action movies, in which brave Moscow tough guys rub out hated *Ukrainian nationalists* as well as *all kinds of black-skinned scum* on the streets of Chicago. In time they once again eat, drink, reflect out loud, once more eat, and then begin exchanging advice about, for example, how to wrap stupid German government officials around their finger, their language – depending on how close they are to passing through Gorlitz – increasingly more often includes somewhat bastardized Germansims (*vonchaim*, they say, *ferzisherung*, and, of course, *finantzamp*), but you can also find out that they won't need to learn the *fascist language – we'll be living in the Russian neighbourhood anyway*. Then comes the time for generalizations about the world, such as *the Germans live well because they work well; but, on the other hand – if we were paid as much as they are, then we would also work well*. New revelations are revealed, one after the other about – how *the Germans truly are a cultured people* and about how *the Germans are kinda stupid and that their humour stinks*. What can you do – Soviet people always were and will be both xenophobes and internationalists at the same time.

Then it's time for jokes, thematically woven, for the most part, around the female sex organ. They don't seem funny to me – I guess I too am kinda stupid and my humour stinks. That's ok, I think to myself, it's ok, I'll put up with all this for just seven or eight hours and then I will be free of you for a whole three months!

(Truth be told, I'm mistaken here: throughout my stay I see these somehow-recognizable faces over and over again and I hear so much

Russian language everywhere I guess that the *fascist one* really does not seem to be necessary here.)

Everything proceeds accordingly: the experienced *people of the PeEMZhe* condescendingly spell out the rules in playing Germaschka, attentive senior citizens (for what reason are they going there, to die?) are ready to believe any nonsense, worried illegal labour migrants (their path runs through Munich to Italy) once again count greenbacks hidden in the most intimate places and, periodically, names, which to me mean something completely different, catch my ear: Florence, Ravenna, Naples . . .

Finally, they stop us at the last border. Beyond is the real Europe, Europe #1, that is, the best that there is in Europe – the Schengen zone, the almost non-existence of borders, the fantastic personified into the real, the freedom of movement.

Our passports are collected by the Poles and then returned by the Germans. We are taken off the bus and are held in *a designated area* for over an hour. Some of the senior citizens nervously look in the direction of the German police – not so much at them as at their German Shepherds. This reminds someone of something. Human thought is associative.

Then a large red-haired policewoman appears with a stack of our passports in her hands. She stands before the entrance to the bus and tells the driver to call us one by one, according to the order our passports are in. Out last names echo their Ukrainian, Russian, and, sometimes, Jewish roots. We return to the bus, also one by one – obediently shout "I!" (or maybe, ja?) upon hearing our last name and then obtain, from the clinging hands of large and sharp Brünnhilde, our personal pass to the world of Woolworth.

The German Gate opens with a slow creak, trumpets blare, the bus, filled to the brim, moves forward.

But there's one thing I cannot understand: what are they going to do later with all those Germans?

2002

Four Million for Our Agents

TRANSLATED BY MARK ANDRYCZYK

"Fine, then," she said, "now I'll ask you too. I'm interested to hear what you'll say about this." She was, I think, an American. Well, she definitely was from New York. Her mission in Ukraine was coming to a close, but she still needed some impressions and conclusions. Before Ukraine, she had visited Mongolia, which, I understood, she found to be more interesting. "Okay," I agreed. "Ask away." The wine was red, the conversation friendly.

"Imagine," she said, "that we give you four million dollars for two years. That's the amount that we give. That is, the amount that we are able to give. What would you do for your country with that sum of money? How would you spend that four million?"

I didn't, of course, answer by joking about a modest house in Switzerland or a small private beach in the Bahamas. Jokes like that are too predictable in our country. That is – they are besmeared by life itself. These aren't really jokes any more. Besides, I am mesmerized by astronomical figures. I have great difficulty imagining this four million in any kind of physical dimension. For me it's like the distance from the Earth to the Sun – to imagine that kind of sum is impossible, so it's best not even to try to imagine it. But, on the other hand, as was said in the film *Amélie*, "the amount of nerve endings in the human brain is a hundred times bigger than the amount of atoms in the Universe."

My nerve endings provided me with the only possible answer: "I don't know, but, in any case, thanks for this topic. I'll try to write something on it."

And this is what I'm now doing.

So, I mentally accept these four million. Let it be some kind of fund, for example. And let it offer stipends. "Give me a stipend, just give me a stipend," Otto von F., the protagonist in my novel *The Moscoviad*, begs. But people like him won't get anything from this fund.

Because these would be stipends for foreigners. So that they could come here, live here for two years, learn the language, translate our writers, get to know our life, travel in our trains, drink our vodka, and smoke our "Pryluky" cigarettes. So that they could discover for themselves all the informal and unofficial sides of our country. So that they could become fascinated with our artists, ideas, our history, our irony, humour, so that they could learn to laugh heartily from our jokes and understand our slang and jargon. So that they wouldn't translate the word "sovok" as "a sandbox shovel" and the phrase "fuck your sausage" as an admission of the completion of an unnatural sexual act with the aforementioned sausage.

So that they – not lastly, but, maybe at the start – would fall in love here. Love relations are the best way to learn a foreign language. After two years of uninterrupted lovemaking, our guests from abroad would attain linguistic virtuosity. Those, who would later proceed and get married with one of our kind would become reliable and stable aides for us, for many years, at least. Those, whose relationships ended in tragic splits, would become more passionate, more devoted, more tender, more sublime individuals.

Of course, they would be a special type of people. The type that doesn't get scared and doesn't loathe. Those, who place the directness of human contact and the patience for understanding above everyday comfort and hygienic sterility. There are enough people like this in the West, among my friends they are a majority. One of them, in a recent letter from Ukraine wrote approximately this: "Who gave me the right to lecture them and to point out to them all those holes and gold teeth? They live as they want to live, because they are at home here, and I can't be right simply because of the fact that I am a traveller here. And most of all, what you can't take away from them is their cuddling vodka warmth. On some kind of extraordinary level, they truly are immeasurably more compassionate than we are. By compassion I mean the tendency to unexpectedly open up, to see in a stranger someone who is dear. It is true that distances of 400–500 kilometres, that our Intercity express trains cover in under four hours, take thirteen hours on their trains. But in those uncomfortable and, as if on purpose, cramped train car compartments people lay out food and drink, get to know one another, share every slice of bread, talk about the most important, sometimes intimate, things. Life's too short – so what's the hurry? Moments of deep, emotional changes, when, out of nowhere, you touch upon the open, vodka-warmth truth are much more important than official-business haste and closed, phony manners, behind which lie emptiness and mutual indifference. I like the fact that they all sometimes seem to be like one giant and endless family that branches out. Having offered their food and vodka to you, they will even become unbearably, relentlessly annoying if you try to reject it. And I don't think it is because food and vodka are relatively cheaper here, but because these people truly have a more honest and giving soul. Thus, rejecting their offer of hospitality is like rejecting their right to be understood. And how different this is from the well-ventilated, perfectly temperature-controlled, deficient of human warmth atmosphere of our steep Eurocity with its superficial sliding smiles and false silence, intruded on only by the crackling of lighters or the rustling of aluminum foil!"

The author of this letter, clearly, doesn't realize that he has already become one of our agents. That's right – an agent of Ukrainian influence, which our culture menacingly and unfairly lacks. No, not an agent of the Ukrainian government, of the regime, of special forces, no way, God forbid, no. But instead, as strange as it may seem, an agent of our poetry, prose, music, history, and agent of our probing and explorations, of our flaws and guffaws.

… And just before their departure, I would lead them along the Chornohora mountain range. So that they'd dream of Ukraine.

2003

A Land of Dreams

TRANSLATED BY MARK ANDRYCZYK

1

I'll dare to begin – I'm not the first and I won't be the last – from a love triangle. This model, it seems, is applicable to everything in the world. For there is love and there is its flip side – what a Russian would term *iznanka* – that is, hate. Everything else is just disguised forms of these two. Actually, aren't these two just disguised forms of one another? In other words, there is just this one thing, some kind of love-hate, Hassliebe, and it displays itself most discernibly in jealousy.

Russians are jealous of the relationship between Ukraine and Poland. Not just those, who to this day consider Ukrainians to be but one tribe within one family-people, the prodigal branch of a lost whole. And not just those, for whom, to this day, so-called Kyivan-Rus remains the cradle of "three brotherly nations" and Kyiv, although it is a word of masculine gender – the mother of all Russian cities. No, if it concerned just those kinds of people, then everything would be fine. But, many times, I've encountered fervent jealousy from Russian "people of dialogue," those impeccable knights of openness, the (as it turned out a bit later) liberal imperialists. "Well what, what will you get out of this Polish expansion?" They ask emotionally. "Don't you see what they are really after?"

One particular example was made up of those, who with a hypertrophic interest, and not without professional engagement, would inquire about "joint projects" – and how much and for what do the Poles give us money, and how often do they visit us, and when they do visit, do they snap photos of train stations, bridges, and other architectural landmarks? Well, these types of people were just fulfilling their duties, in other words, their jealousy was actually the jealousy of their superiors.

By the way, speaking of these superiors – I heard that not too long ago, in Yalta, even an experienced intelligence officer managed to lose his cool; it was brought on by the mere mention of Poles and Ukrainians hosting the European soccer championship together. In response, he kicked his imprudent collocutor from Kyiv with such athletic anger that not only was the European championship now in jeopardy, so was Ukraine's internal championship.

The irritability of that experienced intelligence officer is symptomatic. Russians are irritated by the very fact of the existence of such a rivalry – the fact that they are forced to be jealous of *some silly little Poland*. That is, it is a rather complex *dialectic within the soul*: on the one hand, they cannot help but be jealous, and on the other – they are disgusted by their own jealousy. Because in the eyes of Russians, Poland cannot be considered a worthy rival – if only for the fact that it is not a superpower, like America or China, for example. Moreover, some fifteen years ago, Poland itself was completely dependent on it, on Russia. Poland is but one of those small countries that were once part of the socialist camp. As my acquaintance, a Russian poet, said – *that central European crap*.

But concerning the Ukrainian question, the role of Poland in the thinking of the Russians on foreign-political affairs grows fiercely from the dimensions of an annoying fly to the scale of an elephant, a war elephant. The Russians need this elephant for the verification of one of their most neglected historical myths – the outside, imported *from the-other-side-of-the-hill* nature of "Ukrainian separatism." That is "an ideology of independence" as being an exclusively Galician or perhaps – Western Ukrainian – plot, birthed by all sorts of Austro-European and, most of all Polish, occupants. It is extremely sad to write about all of this again and again because it seemed that this topic was addressed once and for all back then, at the end of the 1980s and beginning of the 1990s. Thus, conceivably, we should forget about it today and instead calmly produce some completely fresh, unexpected geoparabolas. However, the daily political unfolding of Ukrainian-Russian and Ukrainian-Polish relations – above all, the obscenely persistent obsequiousness with which the Ukrainian government barricades itself from everything that is located geographically farther West and submits itself to everything northeastern – forces me to return to old topics that obviously (mea culpa!) have never been fully dealt with and still haven't been exhausted. And it is here that you barely contain yourself from shouting: the hydra has not been crushed! She has grown hundreds of new heads!

2

Are Poles jealous of our relationship with Russia? In other words, why are they still concerned with Ukraine? Unlike Russia, they don't need and never have needed the "Kyivan-Rus" myth for the legitimization of their nation-state – they had plenty of their own. Moreover, even the most chauvinistic of them never allowed themselves to treat Ukrainians as just one particular tribe belonging to "one nation" – except perhaps during the darkest of times, about which, according to Perfetsky,[1] we only know that they once existed. And regarding the idealistic slogan "Without a free Ukraine there is no free Poland" (yet one more echo of the typical Polish saying "For our and your freedom!"), its groundlessness has already been proven even by such poorly informed people as European Commissioners. Could it really be that for them, for the Poles, it simply comes down to the idea that if they finally accept Ukraine in Russia, they will lose a part of their (or, pan-European!) cultural inheritance, which is located *on the other side of the hill*? Could it be that Lviv, Drohobych, and Kremenets, with all of their post-Soviet filthiness to this day are worth this hopeless war, which is predicted to be longer than a 30 Years one? A war, which has the name – "Ukraine's European Choice."

3

When I speak of hopelessness, first of all I have in mind that this really is not a *wojna polsko-ruska pod flagą biało-czerwoną*[2] – we don't know how that one would have ended. Actually, the war between the Russian and the Polish that I have in mind takes place within every average Ukrainian consciousness. That is – it's a war between that consciousness's stereotypes. No, I'm not basing this on any particular social research – it's more like my own internal sociology, the sum of feelings I've assembled through conversations, arguments, observations, disappointments, journeys, media, hearing and smelling, feeling on my skin. So it's a certain *attempt at fictitious sociology*. Its fictitiousness screams of a lack of digital indexes – instead I utilize the vague notion of *an average consciousness*. We can consider this to be just the fancy of a dilettante. Maybe it's just a way of explaining to myself and to others why at least a minimum of three hundred thousand protestor-Ukrainians never took to the streets after their, to be honest, not very popular president gave up yet another part of our gas pipeline network, our independence, our freedom, our pride, to Russia. Something must be sitting there in that *average consciousness* that offers guarantees to that president, the guarantor of the country's independence, that he will get off scot-free.

And so, let's return to stereotypes – the way that I imagine them to be. That is to say, I once again divide a sheet of paper into two vertical halves. Except, this time, on one side I have Poles and on the other – Russians. And, as a result, I find that:

The Russians are straightforward and sincere – the Poles are sly and
   smooth-tongued;
the Russians are large and immense, even in their crimes – the Poles
   are petty and fussy, even in their achievements;
the Russians are considerate, they'll give you the shirt off their back –
   the Poles will probably take it away;
the Russians are Orthodox, *like us* – the Poles are Catholics, they're *Jesuits*;
the Russians are kind-hearted drunks – the Poles are calculated cheapos;
the Russians are *blue collar* – the Poles *white collar*;
the Russians scold, but honestly – the Poles apologize, but bogusly;
the Russians don't encroach upon Ukraine, they want to live in unity
   with it – the Poles encroach upon Ukraine, because they want to
   acquire Lviv;
Poland is located on the other side of the border – Russia is located
   where we are, *in the Union*.

Enough, I am ceasing this rather masochistic exercise, before even completing the first page. Anyone can see that the Russian stereotypes are much more positive. I wonder how much this internal sociology of mine reflects a real one? How devastating would its final results be? And how would it correlate to a comparison of the amount of Russian and Polish films shown on Ukrainian TV channels, to Russian and Polish music on Ukrainian radio? I won't even mention a comparison of Russian and Polish newspapers for sale in Ukrainian kiosks – unlike the local, Ukrainian versions of Russian periodicals such as "Izvestiia v Ukraine" and "Komsomols'kaia Pravda v Ukraine" there is no such thing as the Polish "Gazeta Wyborcza in Ukraine."

To everything above, it is necessary to add the factor of boorish and corrupt border guards, deceptive job finders, and – God forgive! – not very likable, old, loud people with cameras, who have been gathering in Lviv lately en masse, just like masses of their German counterparts do all over Wrocław.

Finally, I will add the ill-fated introduction of the visa requirement by Poles, which in the average Ukrainian consciousness undoubtedly confirms the notion that *they don't really like us and they are only interested in us as a source for cheap labour*.

4

There are more Polonophobes – again, according to what I sense on my skin and under my skin – in Ukraine that there are Polonophiles. The social structure of the former is remarkably wide and diverse. Belonging to it are strata that, perhaps, only on this particular point – polonophobia – cease to be antipodes. Hatred towards Poles could unify any veteran of the UPA with any veteran of the NKVD, if they had ever just once considered discussing this theme. A Ukrainian migrant worker with no rights in Poland could find much in common with an historian-academic of the nomenclatura or even with a former ambassador of Ukraine to Poland.

Polonophiles, on the other hand (and I mean the real ones, not those whose jobs require it), are a rather narrow and clearly defined social group of *agents from the other side of the hill* and enduring demo-liberals, that is, people who came to love Poland and Poles based on their own beliefs and choice, most often a purely aesthetic one: someone heard Niemen or Grechuta in their youth, someone read Lem or Róże-wicz, someone basically memorized Tuwim's "The Ball at the Opera" in Mykola Lukash's translation, someone swallowed up Polish culture in general or, at least, *Kultura* the Polish journal published in Paris. Someone, to this day, flips through Polish illustrated weeklies, that were subscribed to by their parents back in Communist times, someone, to this day, enjoys Mrożek's caricature's on their pages, while someone read *The Castle* for the first time in Polish translation, because finding Kafka in Russian (not to mention in Ukrainian) was utterly hopeless.

Can it be regarded as a society? Undoubtedly – yes. Sometimes I even think that they all know each other personally or, at least, as is to be expected from true agents, that they send signals to one another from afar. Can it be considered to be an influential society, capable of changing the stereotypes of the average consciousness in its own country? I'm not sure. But, otherwise, I don't see any sense in their, our, or my existence.

5

My choice is the same one as theirs, driven by countless invisible and semi-visible threads, but particularly also those that in May 1989 in the Cracow Planty, I was hit in the stomach by a mighty stream coming from a police water cannon – not as a participant, unfortunately, but as an observer of an anti-Soviet demonstration, which for me became a call to rebellion (a personal one, the rebellion of me within me), but even earlier, as a middle-school student, I heard a teacher of Russian language stipulate: *"Don't even think of taking that crap into your hands – those idiotic Polish magazines!"*

and then, somewhat later, as a college student, during lessons of academic communism I heard the professor cluck "Michnik!, Kuroń! Kuroń! Michnik!"

and, in 1994, I met Kuroń, and in 1999, I met Michnik – and this was like a materialization of the spirit of youth, while that professor kept on clucking in his other world,

and it is precisely in that manner, through Poland, over and over again, that I return to the taste, horror, laughter, and insanity of my initiative,

because earlier, when I was a middle-school student, I would listen to Polish radio day and night because it played rock music that wasn't being scrambled,

in other words, in Poland you could do all those things that we couldn't do,

well, almost all,

in other words, out of all this there slowly emerges a certain prohibited conclusion – for example, that we are being fooled in our country – both in that, Soviet one and in this one, which for some reason is regarded as not-Soviet,

that is why, in May 1989, I went to Cracow, to the green poet Mickiewicz, in order to listen to the voices of the dissidents, amplified and distorted by megaphones

and by June already, that is, in a month, I saw how this movement of liberation began reaching us – through those very same megaphones, borrowed from Poland – and I realized that we are moving along the right path,

to tell the truth, to this day I really can't determine: did we deviate from it or is our path that much longer than the Polish one, and everything that took place in the 1990s, truly separated, and not joined, us, even though both we and the Poles, at the same time and equally catastrophically, rid ourselves of romanticism, perhaps, however, in different ways,

because both Poles and we, to be honest, were created by romanticism, and this is very much hopeless,

but, unlike us, they always maintained a critical mass of incorruptible and trustworthy romantic intelligentsia,

and while we were drifting apart throughout those years, I met hundreds of the most exceptional Poles – and these were mostly extremely talented, artistic, plastic, drastic, heretical, and dazzling, and, most often fiery, individuals,

and the amount of vodka I've drunk with them greatly outnumbers the amount I've drunk with Russians, and I've drunk a lot of vodka with Russians,

that's why Poles in the 1990s – are a particular state of mankind,

it's a very young mankind that obtained definitive liberation and impetuously dove into the amphetamine of existence, self-fulfillment, self-enrichment, of life,

I don't know, perhaps they only constitute 0.000001 per cent of the population, but my problem is that I've only met them, that is, I don't know the *real* Poles,

that's why in October 2003, I was so infuriated at the Wrocław airport because of those two border guard bitches, who basically weren't letting me go home,

because throughout those years, for me Poland represented freedom and wherever I would cross its border, I always felt at home,

and even when Poles argued that their country is an ass, I would just shake my head and say, you've never seen a real ass,

because none of my fellow countrymen can deny the sweet and all-encompassing sense of lightness that cloaks each of us as soon as we cross that first border and finally move forward through their, unfamiliar, Polish, territory,

because it's always good to have a land of dreams to the West of you – as an example to follow, or, if not, then and at least as an object of jealousy,

for Poland, that is Germany, for Germany, France, and so forth, because what can be better than France? America?

but Poland is enough for me– from where, everyday, I am asked with despair: "Could this really be the end? Did they really sell you out completely?" – and for some reason it is only the Poles who ask,

and I ask myself once again: Why are they still concerned about this, why are they getting involved again? Do they feel some sense of responsibility for all of us?

Or do they really believe that they'll live to see that day?

2004

The Star Absinthe: Notes on a Bitter Anniversary

TRANSLATED BY MARK ANDRYCZYK

Prypiat is the only city in the world that has such an easily calculated age: 1970 (its founding) – 1986 (its end). Besides that, of all the cities that have been ruined, it existed for the shortest time – only sixteen years. That is, it was no longer a child but not yet a young man, sort of like a teenager who has the right to obtain a passport and to participate in an election for the first time. But, instead of a passport, he is issued a death certificate. And the reason listed for death – Acute Radiation Syndrome.

No other city has existed for such a short time. And it continues to be ruined – usually by human hands. It's not just the forest that eats away at it.

An opportune digression: I wonder – how long did Sodom and Gomorrah exist? You can fantasize about this all you want but it is impossible to imagine that they existed less than Prypiat did. Sixteen years could not have been long enough to bring God to such wrath. In a competition for brevity of existence, Sodom and Gomorrah lag far behind Prypiat.

Moreover, with the example of Prypiat, we have a precise, final date: 27 April 1986. No, not the 26th but the 27th – the day of the evacuation, not of the accident. The existence of an exact, final date makes Prypiat comparable to Pompeii. The latter also has a precise date – 24 August 79.

The ghost of Pompeii climbed up out of nowhere into reality when we, stepping onto broken glass and rotten boards, lifting our feet like herons, entered the Prypiat Café – at one time the coolest joint in town. The café was situated on a hill above the river docks. From there you can observe the city's beach and the arrival of the blindingly white Kyiv passenger liners with their underwater wings. The wall of the café across from the beach was made of stained glass. Our Guide took the opportunity to share with us the fact that, according to lore, the artist who had made this stained glass wall had, at one time, created another stained glass piece that tempted fate. What he had in mind was that, among other works by that stained-glass artist, there was "The Last Day of Pompeii." He did indeed curse this place. There's no way a person like that should have been asked to create any stained glass in Prypiat. Our Guide chuckled while telling us this legend.

It's doubtful that "The Last Day of Pompeii" could have become a monumental-decorative theme during, need I remind you, a time of Socialist Realism – not even as a replica of Karl Briullov's work. What club, hall, or sanatorium could have had any use for its catastrophism? What executive committee could have ordered a far-from-the-most-optimistic scene depicting volcanic lava and the scorn of the heavens?

One can perhaps understand a moment of the artist's weakness that resulted in a work being given birth to out of wedlock. A stained glass work made for oneself? In order to materialize random apocalyptic visions? Art that does not belong to the people? Art for art's sake? In any case, that latent decadent categorically should not have been invited to Prypiat. People like him always drag their horrible karma around with them and meddle into otherwise happy streams of events.

Where can he be found today, how can he be made responsible for everything that came to be?

What's on the stained glass?

For starters it's worth noting that almost half of it was ruined. That is, today, it's no longer a stained glass work, but half of one, only pieces of it remain intact. The other half crackles underfoot when you carelessly come too close to it. By the way: upon entering the café, the radiation metre strapped to Our Guide's shoulder began to flap madly, alerting us to a dangerous hot spot. We carefully circumvented it. You can't walk barefoot here – you'll be overexposed.

So then, getting back to the stained glass. Everything that has remained gives the sense of an accented splash of colours. If one were to describe the colours of the stained glass in terms of physics, you would need to use the prefixes "infra-" and "ultra-" as much as possible. The stained glass is remarkably active, it emits. The verb "to emit" usually requires an object in the accusative case. You can emit something, for example, happiness. Or radiation. The stained glass in the Prypiat Café on the shores of the Prypiat River in the city of Prypiat simply emits.

Its sun is multi-coloured. Like the rest of the world, it's striped. The stripes are dark-red, bright yellow, blue, azure, and green. This is summer in all its fury, at its zenith, in its surplus – the singing of forests, the silence of lakes, reeds, pines, the buzzing of bubble bees among the bushes of berries, becoming one with nature, the sweet swelling of the biosphere.

A bit later, when we were already in the bus, Our Guide played an agitprop film for us about Nuclear Power Plants (NPP) that was filmed the previous summer, that is, the last summer before the catastrophe. "And what's most important," a choleric guy with the rank of an engineer, in a white lab coat and glasses said in one scene, all choked up by his own enthrallment – "what's most important: we live in such unity with nature here, we are the flesh of its flesh! Go swim in the river, enter the forest, walk among the pines, breath, gather a whole frying-pan-full of mushrooms for dinner, if you want, it's all here, right next to you, we are in it, we are part of it."

About nine months later – and this fidgety, life-embracing person, with his quick manner of speech seemed cruel. But for now – the propaganda of success, the standard victorious context in which the words "man" and "nature" are now always written in uppercase letters, M and N, Man and Nature, NatureMan, a celebration of harmony, swimming in the river, gathering mushrooms, the peaceful atom,[1] the scent of pine, dialectic materialism.

The inhabitants of Prypiat exemplified the success of scientific communism, they embodied it – clean, naive, and obtrusive.

Are you really sure that instead of "obtrusive" I should have written "cocky"?

Most unforgettable that day were, of course, the catfish in the canal near the Nuclear Power Plant. They were the size of dolphins, or sharks, and this is nature's categorically harsh answer to man (now in a different context – one in which both of these words are always written in lowercase letters).

Gazing at fish in water is one of my favourite and constant activities. I've had very few opportunities to do this in my life. One, for example, came in Nuremberg, another – in Regensburg. I think it was in Nuremberg that I came to the conclusion that Europe is a land in which fish live well. I would not have come to this conclusion if I hadn't been in Nuremberg precisely at that time, in the summer of 1995. If I hadn't stood on those bridges time and again and I hadn't gazed down deep into the river to see how fish slowly move just above its bottom. And I ended up in Nuremberg at that time just because Walter Mossmann summoned us to come there.

And now I am recalling him not just casually, and not out of thanks but because, a few months earlier, he too gazed at those very same catfish in the canal near the Nuclear Power Plant. In his report he writes about "metre-long monstrosities with giant, flat skulls and wide jaws, and with long, waving outgrowths jutting from the left and the right of their jaws that recall the curled moustaches of the Zaporozhian Cossacks."

That's a rather caustic joke, in case anyone missed it: catfish with Cossack moustaches in a radioactive canal nestled in slime and sluggish, the cold blood of Ukraine, its adipose fish hearts.

Europe? A land in which fish live well?
It's doubtful – in the case of those catfish.
First of all, I'm not sure if they really live all that well. But they definitely live long: no one catches them or kills them, in fear of the undeniable danger of radiation. How long is Silurus glanis, a normal (non-radioactive) Wels Catfish, supposed to live? According to several sources – up to one hundred years. This fish can live longer than any other fish found in our rivers and waters. Only moss-covered carp can live longer – but that's only in Aldous Huxley's novels.

On the other hand, abnormal (radioactivus emanatos) catfish – that is, the Prypiat catfish – live eternally. And as evidenced by their size in the twenty-fifth year of their eternal life after the catastrophe, they will continue to grow eternally. And someday they'll grow into eternally living monstrous leviathans. But will they really be living well then?

Second of all, I'm not sure if it's really Europe. In our country Europe occasionally appears and then disappears again. It's phantasmic, like communism in the early poetry of Marx-Engels. You can't touch it, it's made of mist, misunderstandings, and rumours.

In April 1986 Europe was not even a topic of discussion. There was the USSR and there was the West and also China. What Europe? Central? Eastern? If "Eastern" then how can you call that Europe? Europe cannot be eastern. From our geography lessons we learned that there is only the European territory of Russia and a few adjacent republics. The city of Prypiat was located somewhere there in that European territory. But certainly not in Europe.

And really – if it wasn't for Sweden, if it hadn't created such a ruckus about the accident then how would this have continued on? There probably would not have been any continuation, just another cover-up of yet another mega-crime. They nonetheless classified as secret the oncological illness statistics, regardless of all those Swedes. What, do you think the USSR was going to change all of a sudden?

And it's good that there was a resistance to the system. It's good that Sweden made a fuss and indicated that Poland was in danger. It's good that Poland had stopped being a friend and was increasingly turning away, westward. This time it turned away from a radioactive cloud – holding its breath and fastidiously holding its nose. It's good that Poland became frightened and took up Sweden's appeal.

But France did not stop being a friend and denied everything. There is no danger, France said, there is nothing to see here. It's a good thing the European Union didn't exist then. Otherwise it would have, once again, come up with some kind of blushingly indecisive decision (please excuse the oxymoron) – like the one they came up with during the war in Georgia – the most important thing is not to anger the Russians.

It's good that Germany had had the experience of the 1970s, when hundreds of thousands and even millions of people protested against the nuclear power plants, led by a few poets with guitars and fifes. It's good that by 17 May 1986 the German Greens called an emergency meeting in Hannover. And it was on 17 May that I wrote these lines

Blood will change. Blossoms will fall from the chestnut trees.
We rush to live, like after a plague.
Perhaps that is where salvation lies – to recognize this time,
as a final flowering. The Only. One.

No one understood what they were about. On the other hand, Walter Mossmann, who certainly would have understood, did not know about their existence. "And then I tried," he writes about that day, "to imagine an infected landscape, forests, pools of water, fields, villages – everything is radiating. And I wasn't able to. This is not something that can be seen in reality."

I replied to him a dozen years later: "What were our initial reactions? To understand them is to understand what it is to fear the wind, the rain, the greenest of grass, to be afraid of light." And later – concerning the presence of a different kind of death – one that you cannot sense or see, "death to grow into,[2] death so devoid of form (and, following Hegel – content), that any kind of resistance lost any sense."

But the authorities demanded that resistance be applied. They, from the first days, shamelessly hurled full echelons of poor souls rescuers into the Zone – the same way, as if in war time, they hurled, *full speed ahead*, masses of un-uniformed and unarmed men from the "recently liberated territories." The authorities were in charge of the resistance and were bringing about their own end. But no one had realized it at that time. It seemed that the end of the world would come sooner than the end of such a wonderful epoch-empire.

The resistance consisted of de-activization. Zone X was ordered to be washed of its dirt. What couldn't be washed was to be buried in the ground.[3] What could not be buried was to be left as it was.

But there was another resistance as well, which consisted of pillaging. It's as if people decided to deal with the radioactivity of the materials through the act of dividing the loot, that is, through the acquisition of things that belong to others. It's as if someone's possessions, when taken out of their home, immediately lose their deathly glow.

That's why Prypiat is a city not only abandoned but also a city robbed, a take-out city, a city taken apart, a city to go. And that is its particular attraction. No longer a city but a body, collectively raped by new gangs of rescuers-lovers each time.

In his notes on Prypiat, Walter Mossmann calls it "an installation beyond compare." I also couldn't shake the feeling sometimes that all this surrounding me was probably a fragment of an exposition that had been especially created and then methodically developed inside some kind of Contemporary Art-and-Ecology Zone – it's just that the curators overdid it and now the dose-metre goes bonkers in some places. And not just they – that very same Walter Mossmann admits a bit later: "The entire city of Prypiat is an installation with such a rich Bedeu-tungsebenen[4] that it creates buzzing in your skull."

Picking up on his skull buzzing, I attempt to list at least the highest "levels of meaning" – as if trying to formulate a question about the semiotics of Prypiat. I've even come up with more than two levels. Here are just the first five:

Ecological
Political

Social
Lyrical
Mythological

In the case of the last one, it emerges – a friend of the people and an enemy of the gods, a superman and near-god himself, that is – a titan.

It was Prometheus, and not Sabaoth or Jehovah, who created man from clay. What word first comes to mind when we hear his name? Correct – "fire." But it should be "clay," one that is red, at least. The meaning behind the fire that was stolen from the gods for man can only be understood if the factor of clay is taken into consideration – that is, the condition that Prometheus needed to care for those that he had fashioned out of clay. By the way, I hear in the Ukrainian word for "burn" (*o-pik*) the root of the word for "to care for" (*pik-luvatysia*). Clay hardens and strengthens as a result of burning. There is no way to avoid fire here. If fire burns in a nuclear reactor, then all the more so.

Prometheus is a favourite of the Romantics, it is they who, one after another, as if according to plan, sang of his self-sacrificial protest against the static order of things. It is not strange that Shevchenko, in his "The Caucasus," a poem that is first and foremost concretely political, launches it with him, bound to the top of a cliff for thirty thousand years (well that's a long sentencing!). And an eagle fits in here too – not necessarily a two-headed one but an autocratic devourer of a liver nonetheless.

Prometheus remained a favourite in the era of Socialist Realism as well – in the sphere of late Soviet electro-energy. He was sort of a patron of more and more electro-stations and of the residential areas tied to them. It is as if he came up with the slogan about the electrification of the whole country.

It's understood that Prypiat could not help but be one of the centres of this cult. Yet another blow from greedy and lascivious gods landed on the reactor.

Second, of course, a star or, more accurately, the Star called Wormwood. We began to actively quote verses 10 and 11 from chapter 8 of St John the Divine's Revelation in the summer of 1986, that is, about a month after the catastrophe. Wormwood is a very strange, a completely ridiculous, name, if one really has a star in mind – and even if by star one has in mind a comet or an asteroid. Why should a cosmic body have the same name as a field plant? It only begins to make sense when taking into account the place where the catastrophe occurred.

In that manner, wormwood is a double "a": apocalypse and absinthe. Both are extracts of sorts: the former – of a secret knowledge, the latter – of bitterness. If geographical names were to be translated then discussions on an international level would not be about the ChNPP (the Chernobyl Nuclear Power Plant) but about the ANPP (the Absinthe Nuclear Power Plant). They would be about a technogenic catastrophe not in Chornobyl but in Absinthe.

There is, of course, a third "a" – angel (yes, the third one, the one who sounded the trumpet). Isn't that whom we see among other figures on the aforementioned stained glass in that café in what is yet another allusion to Pompeii made by the artist? The angel, although disguised as a flying girl (with breasts!), and although with invisible wings, is nonetheless given a trumpet as its main and most important sign. Angels cannot have female sexual organs, moreover primary ones, because angels are sexless. But angels can pretend to be girls. Long hair and the absence of indicators of the male sex, even secondary ones, allow for this. That angel flying on that stained glass window, perhaps, is one like that. Its author didn't really know but was trying to guess. And sometimes a guess is much more impressive than actual knowledge.

We drove down Lenin Avenue to get to the City of the Electric Sun. We exited the bus on the main square in front of the Energy-Man Palace of Culture, where Lenin Avenue intersected Kurchatov Street. Actually, the epithet "former" needs to be used everywhere in these sentences – at least six or seven times. "Former" is the primary and most important characteristic of Prypiat. It makes you kick in your memory, full on. Memory has to work for everything else because nothing else remains in Prypiat.

When I was a kid I often dreamt about the Yucatán and about cities abandoned in jungles. And although to compare Prypiat with it seems too flattering, and thus dishonest, I do compare them. It's about how nature, upon returning, takes back its own. It's about weeds, sometimes impassible, in former courtyards, about trees on the roof and on stairs, about boars or deer, that suddenly cross Friendship of Peoples Avenue (formerly: now, today – Friendship of Animals). It's about extraterrestrial and hypertrophic mushrooms filled to their caps with roentgens. Nature returned and took back a hundredfold, unnaturally. The indifferent-merciless revenge of nature against the system can attest to the unnatural quality of that system. To the notion that the place where Kurchatov and Lenin intersect goes beyond the boundaries of the order of things and is horribly dangerous.

The contamination was worst in the park. It was best not even to approach the Ferris wheel. According to Our Guide the park missed its own opening by just four days. The opening was to take place on 1 May, everything stood, just about ready, all the carousels *greased and ready to go*, all that was left to do was wave a hand, signal the orchestra, cut the red ribbon, and give the command. The inhabitants of Prypiat were methodically getting their kids ready: ten, nine, eight, seven, six, five days until the opening!

That was approximately the amount of days left for the existence of communism. This was evidenced by prosperity, its growth, and by the Kyiv Cakes, for which people from Kyiv would come to Prypiat. Stepping onto the broken glass and other screeching scraps I could not help but notice the countless ranges and refrigerators in the "Rainbow" store. Well there it is, embodied in the consumer goods – this *higher*, this truly highest, as if in Moscow, category of supply!

The chief colour for the city of Prypiat should have been the colour of those ranges, refrigerators, and washing machines – an ideally white colour, the sum total of the rainbow, an indicator of the inability to get dirty or stained, an index of absolute cleanliness and sterility, the colour of lab coats, wings, orchards in late April, and rapid passenger liners with under-water – also white – wings, that arrived at the city docks, one after the other.

And if we imagine the angels clothed, then it is also the colour of their special clothing.

That's why, when I walked around inside the former Energy-Worker Palace I could not help but think about the third myth and, simultaneously, the phantom, of this city. His name is Harmonious Man – an exemplary creation of Prometheus, clay creation No 1, the tireless, conscientious worker, a dazzling dancer, the blessed-with-perfect-pitch-and-velvety-voiced champion of the world in chess and swimming and also in acrobatics, numismatics and gymnastics. On a heavily peeling panel in the foyer of the palace hall, the exemplary Workers, Engineers, and Scientists united in a new Trinity with the exemplary Villagers and embraced each other in a happy round dance. The concert hall continued to echo something from Leontiev, Antonov, maybe some Rotaru, her "Lavanda"[5] and other songs.

A bit later, in the workshop beside the palace, filled with portraits of members of the Politburo, I tried to recall their last names. In the army we had to know them by heart in order to distinguish between their identically kind, good faces. But how can you distinguish between Voronov and Kapitonov? Ustinov and Tikhonov? Gromyko and Kunaev? Or, even more difficult, how can you tell the difference between Vorotnikov and Solomentsev? How can you tell the difference between the ideal and the ideal? Between the positive and the positive? Between the perfect and the harmonious? Between the good and the even better?

The city of Prypiat died because of the inability to answer these questions. The Harmonious Man could not withstand his own progress and choked on happiness.

P.S. I also remember something else that Our Guide told us. In the days before the 1986 New Year's holiday, the holiday tree in front of the Energy-Worker Palace fell down twice. Few of the city's inhabitants paid any attention to such a telling sign.

March 2011

Love and Hatred in Kyiv[1]

TRANSLATED BY VITALY CHERNETSKY

It has been severely cold here lately, with temperatures dipping below freezing night after night. What sustains the protesters at Independence Square in weather this bleak can only come from inside: an exceptionally hot mix of despair, hope, self-sacrifice, and hatred.

Yes, hatred. Morality does not forbid hating murderers. Especially if the murderers are in power or in direct service of those in power – with batons, tear gas, water cannons, rubber bullets, and, starting 22 Jan., live ammunition.

That day, the news came about the first two protesters to be shot and killed by the police since the protests began in November. One of them, Serhiy Nihoyan, a 20-year-old Ukrainian of Armenian heritage, dreamed of becoming an actor. The other, Mikhail Zhiznevsky, a citizen of Belarus, was also young, just 25 years old. An ethnic Armenian and a Belarusian, giving their lives for the freedom of Ukrainians – this gives the lie to the fears, held by some in the West, that the democracy movement here is being hijacked by Ukrainian nationalists.

If anyone is promoting hatred it is the government. My friend Josef Zissels, chairman of the Association of Jewish Organizations and Communities of Ukraine, and vice president of the World Jewish Congress, wrote a few days ago that the website of Berkut, the special police force (and a final line of defence for the powers that be) had been "flooded with anti-Semitic materials that allege that the Jews are to blame for organizing at Maidan," the central square, which has become synonymous with the protests.

Mr Zissels wrote: "This is completely absurd, but those who are armed with batons and shields, now facing the protesters, believe this. They are brainwashed into believing that the Maidan is a Jewish project, and thus there is no need to take pity on anyone – you can beat them all."

Beat them all. The police have beaten women and children, and even priests trying to intervene to stop the bloodshed. Berkut not only beats; it maims, tortures, and kills. Its members like to pounce on individuals who have gotten separated from the crowd of protesters. Some have even posed for the cameras, their boots on the heads of victims lying on the ground. They proudly upload these photos and videos to their personal pages at social networking sites.

Article 21 of our Constitution states that "human rights and freedoms shall be inalienable and inviolable."

The abuses by the ruling authorities, and their escalating use of violence, have threatened to make the Constitution a joke.

On 16 Jan., the government of President Viktor F. Yanukovych pushed through Parliament a package of laws severely curtailing freedom of speech and assembly. This week, the prime minister resigned, and the majority of the repressive laws were repealed, partly because of the wave of international condemnation.

It is precisely for their rights and freedoms – long and brazenly violated by the Yanukovych regime – that the Ukrainian people are now fighting. They have been given no other choice. Our national anthem says, "We will lay down our body and soul for our freedom." On 19 Jan., the protests turned violent. But if no one resists the riot police, the thinking goes, Ukraine will be turned into one large prison in a matter of weeks.

This is why an acquaintance of mine, a translator of Kierkegaard and Ibsen, now spends her time making Molotov cocktails, and her young sons, classics majors, aged 17 and 19, throw their mother's products in the direction of the wall of smoke on Hrushevsky Street, which runs past major government buildings.

This is why an 80-year-old Kyiv grandmother brought her knitting needles to the protest headquarters and gave them to the first protester she saw with the words, "Take them, son. If you don't kill the monster, maybe you'll at least stop it."

This is why even the Hare Krishnas in Kyiv now carry baseball bats.

We are defending ourselves, our country, our future, Europe's future – some with Molotov cocktails, some with knitting needles, some with paving stones, some with baseball bats, some with texts published on the Internet, some with photos documenting the atrocities.

The police have been targeting journalists as rabidly as they have targeted medics taking the wounded out of the scene of clashes. Berkut has been treating journalists with cameras and notebooks as the enemy. Several dozen journalists have been wounded, hit by stun grenades, tear gas, or rubber bullets.

Recently, coordinators of the protest made an appeal across online social networks for medicine and diapers – which are excellent at absorbing blood. The people of Kyiv began bringing drugs and nappies to the protest headquarters on such a scale that in just a few hours a new message went up online: "Enough medication for now! We don't have enough storage space! But we urgently need warm clothes, bread, tea and coffee!" And again, people from all over Kyiv brought everything they could to help.

The authorities can't understand this. Recently, some unknown thugs in civilian clothes kidnapped an activist and spent the night torturing him, demanding: Who is funding the Maidan? Which Western sources? Is it the State Department, or someone else?

The regime's mental system of coordinates cannot fit one simple fact: The Maidan funds itself, through its own love and its own hatred.

I have never loved my homeland as much as I love it now. Before, I had always been sceptical and restrained towards it. I am 53 years old, and had long put sentimentality behind me.

But these days I see our women, young and old, sorting with amazing efficiency the donated medications and food supplies, I see hipster students in hockey masks and camouflage pants fearlessly going onto the frontline barricades, I see our workers and farmers providing security for the Maidan protesters, our grannies and grandpas who keep bringing more and more hot food to Independence Square, and I feel a lump in my throat.

January 2014

Seven Hundred Fierce Days, or the Role of a Contrabass in the Revolution

TRANSLATED BY MARK ANDRYCZYK

1
Pre-History

Even in times of peace, the lives of wandering actors are full of trials and dangers. Not a bad opening phrase, if I say so myself.

Back in late October, the entire "Albert" troupe gathered in Ivano-Frankivsk. Once, not too long ago, but long ago nonetheless, I came upon the story of a man whose name was Albert Wyrozemsky and who was publically burned alive in Lviv in 1641. The tale was only a few sentences long so I decided to expand it in order to turn it into a short story. I wrote it right away.

Albert Wyrozemsky was burned alive because he "partook in the most heinous act by a human in the entire history of the city" – he sold out to the Devil. Serving a sentence in an underground cell in the Bernardine Monastery he wrote on the wall with his own blood that he was ready to give up his soul to hell. And that is what the short story is about, but not only about that.

After a few years, "Albert" was taken on by a small group of very talented people: Olya, Ulyana, Anatoly, Mark. No, this was not a coincidence. Olya read it first, in such a way that she found room in it for Ulyana's voice, movement, and gestures, Anatoly's black and white drawings, and Mark's upright bass.

Both room and space.

In this way, sometimes with difficulty, sometimes with amazing ease, we began giving birth to the theatrical-literary-musical-multimedia performance "Albert, or The Highest Form of Execution." We presented it at three different festivals, in three completely different situations.

At the ArtPole festival in Unizh we played in the middle of a July night under the stars accompanied by the crackling embers of a truly live fire, which sounded like the crunching of broken bones.

At the Meridian Czernowitz Festival we performed to a standing-room-only crowd in the Schiller-Kobylianska theatre[1] – a building so glamorous that during the day while we were rehearsing, one young couple after another came by to pose in front of it for their wedding photos.

At the GogolFest festival we performed in a Kyiv industrial area, in a building that is now referred to as a cinema hall. Rain misted and autumn leaves poured in through holes in the roof, on us and onto the stage, and I won't even mention the appearance of two doves, one black, one white.

And so, at the end of October, over several days, we reworked and altered our performance, adding new episodes and lyrical asides. All of this was being done with a future tour in mind. We agreed that it was to take place in the second half of February. Perhaps in seven cities, perhaps in nine, in the West, East, South and, of course, in the capital.

Back then, at the end of October, none of us could have imagined that massive protests would soon begin in Ukraine. Moreover, we couldn't predict that, precisely in the second half of February, the Euromaidan protests would reach a bloody culmination.

2
The Beginning of the Story

I came to Kyiv for the Euromaidan on 1 December 2013, on a day featuring one of the most intense protests, caused by unprecedented (then still unprecedented) animalistic violence unleashed against the protestors on the night before 30 November. This was the beginning of the war that the Yanukovych regime would wage against all of us. The capital, and all of Ukraine, countered this brutal and bloody attempt at instilling fear with one million protesters. I really needed to be among them.

From that day, I remained in Kyiv for almost all of December. I will never forget how on the night before the 11th, we ran to the Maidan from various directions in order to defend it from being stormed, in great numbers, with a living mass of people. During those nights and days we hadn't yet donned helmets and other defensive weapons. All we had were our bodies. If we could achieve a critical mass of people, then we could rescue the Maidan. That is what we understood our assignment to be. On the night before the 11th, that is precisely the way we were able to halt their attack – in just a few hours there were already several tens of thousands of us. The bells of St Michael's Church rang throughout Kyiv, and there was something archetypical and medieval about that.

On one of the following days, 14th December to be precise, all of us "Alberts" met up in front of the re-established barricade on Instytutska Street. Olya wanted to hear from each of us if we hadn't decided to cancel our February tour *because of the circumstances*. It was to start in just two months but it was clear that the situation was not going to change by then, that the Euromaidan would still be standing. Well, unless they'd start using flame-throwers and tanks against it. But that would then signify the end of the world. Not just the end of our projects, stories, poems, songs, productions and visions, but the physical end of all of us.

We unanimously decided to resist that perspective and to continue on with our plans no matter what. Right there, in front of the barricade on Instytutska Street we recorded a video in which each of us talked about the unexpected appropriateness of "Albert," about black and white, about the forces of the night, who suspend their attack at dawn. And then attack again at night.

It was then that we finalized our tour schedule: from the 18th to the 25th – Ivano-Frankivsk, Ternopil, Kyiv, Zaporizhzhia, Odesa. Five cities in total. Although we had talked about doing nine. But then there were contrary plans to cancel the whole thing. So even five was not too bad. Thus, nothing came of the contrary plans: art and revolution would walk side by side. No revolution would *cancel* art, if only because it thrives on its ideas and emotions. And the converse is true – no art would cancel a revolution because it is always balancing somewhere on the border of the future.

Today I had the notion that the entire week, between the 19th and the 25th of February, was not really seven days long but seven hundred. We also didn't cancel any of the performances because those who had shot at our friends in the centre of Kyiv, who didn't just shoot at them but aimed at and hit their hearts, eyes, or groins, had just that in mind, the cancelling – of performances, lives, human dignity, courage, creativity, resistance. "It's hard to believe that we began in complete darkness – an hour before the storming of the Maidan," Olya wrote in yesterday's letter.

What follows are a few fragments from those days.

3
Franyk

On February 18th the strange, feigned truce ended and a fatal confrontation had renewed. The government forces named this operation "Boomerang." They lured a large crowd of protestors – mostly peaceful participants of the so-called peaceful offensive, including women, who were without shields and helmets, not even wooden ones – to move towards the parliament building and then counterattacked them with great force and from various directions. Just past noon they moved up close to the Maidan, taking down barricades and further beating up the injured along the way. And not just beating them up more, but doing it with a particular cruelty. Who among us has not heard about the headless body in Mariinsky Park? By 6 p.m. the Maidan had been surrounded by a strangling, tight circle. In the coming hours the worst was supposed to come – complete annihilation.

At 7 p.m. we opened our performance with a moment of silence.

The storming began a few minutes after eight. Right then we were performing the final stanza of Bohdan Ihor Antonych's poem "The Trumpets of the Final Day." The final stanza of the final day. We were the only ones in the hall that didn't know: it had begun. When our show soon came to an end, the public stood up and applauded with particular gusto. As if also for one final time. The perimeter of the Maidan was already in flames at that moment. This was the last hope for its defenders – that impenetrable curtain of smoke made by burning tires, wood, rags, and everything lying nearby. That fire was despair.

And that night too I saw how the building of the SBU (Security Service of Ukraine) in my city was burning. It was once the building of the KGB. It was once, if I am not mistaken, the building of the Gestapo. I decided that the sight of that itself made holding out until this night of despair worth it.

The Kyiv Maidan somehow managed to make it through that night.

4
Ternopil

The next day we travelled by bus to Ternopil. The bridge that cars would use to cross the Dnister River in Nyzhniv was controlled by a checkpoint manned by the city's self-defence group. It is in times like that you realize that large bridges over large rivers are indeed strategic.

Villagers from Nyzhniv, armed with poles and, it seemed, pitchforks, made sure that no unit of the government forces could advance on Kyiv from the west. I have no doubt they would have lain down in front of any government vehicles.

On the other hand, alongside us, one bus after another sped ahead filled with rebellious people. Yet again, for those few months of the revolution, people dropped everything and came together to defend the Maidan. Some of them died the very next day – having arrived there for the first and last time.

In Ternopil, we began our rehearsal but had to interrupt it. The city's stage crew asked us to. Captured members of the Berkut special police force were to walk down in a procession along Shevchenko Boulevard, on which the theatre was located. Everyone wanted to see this triumph of the rebellious people over the hated pigs. In besieged medieval cities this is how they led their enemies, tarred and feathered, down corridors of shame. I still don't know if those Ternopil Berkut guys had been captured or if they voluntarily had switched sides. It was probably a mix of the two. They were led in a column along the city's central boulevard, unarmed, and humiliated. Their shields and helmets became trophies. Their bus was covered in revolutionary slogans.

After our performance we once again received a standing ovation. That evening, a candle, lit in the final scene, didn't seem prosaic at all.

At night, after the performance, we boarded the train to Kyiv and settled into our compartments. But we didn't go anywhere. The train didn't move for an hour, then two. Rumours that the train route from Western Ukraine to Kyiv was blocked had been confirmed. The government feared that the Maidan would be replenished with more and more protestors. The official reason for the disruption of rail travel *for an undesignated amount of time* was "the washing out of the train tracks in the Teteriv-Korosten area."

We fell asleep in the motionless train nonetheless.

At 8 a.m. the conductor told us to leave the train. He had just been told that Kyiv was not going to happen. The train would stay in Ternopil until the following night and would then return to Chernivtsi. "I'd strangle that crook with my bare hands," the conductor said with a thick Bukovynian accent. It was crystal clear whom he had it mind.

Above all else, we needed to continue on our way. It's a good thing that our Kyiv performance, sold out now for about ten days, was not scheduled until the following evening.

We went from the Ternopil train station, with all our things and the upright bass, to the Koza Art Bar. That morning it served as peculiar mix of revolutionary headquarters, an information centre, and a base for mobilization. Smaller groups who would try to get to Kyiv by car or bus were assembling there. In the meantime, everyone watched live Internet broadcasts from the Maidan on a large screen.

The Ukrainian language has the phrase "to fall, like a sheaf." Here, our ancient village mentality once again lets itself be known. "Like a sheaf" is equal to "as if mowed down." Ulyana was calling someone. Our guys on Instytutksa Street were, in her word, falling like sheaves. Enemy snipers, who were methodically shooting them down from one of the highest floors of the Ukraina Hotel, were characterized by two different calling cards: one always hit the heart, and the other the carotid artery. The numbers of killed and fatally wounded were growing every minute. Many were shot and killed while attempting to pull a friend's body away from the shooting zone. To load a body on yourself to carry it away, you had to lay down your shield, exposing yourself. Those few seconds were all the snipers needed.

February 20th – was the day of the most intense concentration of the regime's evil deeds. Those killed would soon come to be known as the Heavenly Hundred.

It was hardest on Yulia. She was a volunteer from Vinnytsia, who worked during all the months of the Maidan – every day and night she would work in the medical unit. That day she had been put in charge of the telephones. The cell phones of The Slain Ones were brought to her, they formed a very long row – right in front of her eyes. Her responsibility was to answer calls made to those who were no longer alive. Yulia looked with horror at all those silent Nokias and Samsungs. Then they began to ring, one after another. Most heartbreaking was when the phone screen lit up with the word "MOM."

5
The Road to Kyiv

It wasn't until several hours later that we set off for Kyiv. The good people from the Koza Art Bar found us a compact little bus with room for seven. We packed ourselves into it together with our eighth friend, the upright bass.

Our driver's son had been wounded on the Maidan that morning. "I'll take you there and then I'm bringing back my son," the man said.

But not so fast! "Dad," his son replied over the phone, "I'm fine: a few shell fragments in my thigh, and in my shoulder. I'm staying – I'm not going anywhere. Take some of the other guys, they're worse off."

And how can we not triumph with these kinds of people on our side?

I recall a very long line of ambulances on the Zhytomyr road between Rivne and Kyiv, about ten of them. Kyiv needed more of them, and Rivne was less than four hours away. And people say there are no more real doctors in this country?!

All the roads to Kyiv had been cleared by now; the traffic police had scattered. We did see increasingly larger checkpoints manned by self-defence groups. People were able to organize themselves in just a few hours, tearing their land back from the power of the regime, right in front of our eyes.

In situations such as these the word "we" becomes something much larger – WE.

6
Kyiv

On 21 February, we (the smaller "we," our theatre troupe) finished our rehearsal at the Molodyi Theatre and headed down to Khreshchatyk Street. Topographically, this was Khreshchatyk Street but, in a wider sense, it was the Maidan, its territory, a city within a city. The last time I had been there was a week ago, during the so-called truce. The difference was astonishing. After those last, most difficult days and nights, it had become horribly blackened – the sidewalks, the walls, the trees, the faces of people. It seemed that black dust had so deeply eaten into these features, cracks, and scars, that it would never be washed away. It was as if coalminers from Donetsk had come out en masse onto the Maidan straight out of coalmines, without washing up after their shifts. But in camouflage, for some reason, and definitely not in their coalminers' helmets.

Yes, the fire. That is what burned everything it could reach. Fire, smoke, ashes, wind, and soot. Fire, that burned down any final bridges of compromise.

There were almost no cobblestones remaining underfoot. They were called the weapon of the proletariat at one time.

Two open caskets with The Slain Ones were carried past us. A countless number of passers-by stopped, took off their hats and made the sign of the cross. In reality, that evening should have been spent searching for caskets for tomorrow's solemn burial – an entire hundred heavenly caskets.

Once more we began our performance with silence. And later, after the show, we once again received passionate applause. Anatoly said that he couldn't hold back his tears. Yulia, that same woman who was a volunteer with the medical unit, walked up; she was with Volodymyr, a Kyivan who, like Yulia, had been on the Maidan for all three months, and who had spent the last few weeks mostly supplying it with tires. "It seems to me," he was commenting on the performance, "the message is that no matter what price you sell your soul for, you'll sell it too cheap."

I decided that, perhaps, that indeed is how it is. In other words, our performance is about the fact that it's impossible to sell your soul. I finally realized this myself and couldn't believe that I, the author, couldn't fathom this earlier. I needed an intermediary for this. Or a messenger. This stranger Volodymyr, the lord of the tires.

7
Kyiv (continued)

On 22 February I almost died from joy. Dmytro called me in the morning and offered *a tour of Mezhyhiria*.[2] Just before New Year's, Dmytro and I, a bunch of friends, and another ten thousand or so protestors had already rushed over there to try and open a quick, second front right at the gate of The Cannibal. Back then, all the roads and approaches had been closed off by the internal police, behind which stood the Berkut, behind which stood some other troops dressed in black – the last line of defence, refined natural killers, Tonton Macoutes.

On 22 February they were all gone. They scattered, ran away, melted away, disappeared, died – as if they had never existed. Mezhyhiria stood open and defenceless – with all of its legendary ostriches, camels, Greek ruins, exotic plants and birds, paintings looted from museums, golden loafs of bread and WC pans, with all those things that they hadn't managed (didn't want?) to take with them. And without Yanukovych.

Yanukovych ran away?! The revolution has triumphed?!

I tried to calm my crazed and ready-to-explode-at-any-second heart with all my might, gulping down a hypernormal amount of corvalol pills. It would have been unfair and just plain wrong if it had stopped beating on that particular day.

8
Zaporizhzhia

It didn't calm down until I was on the overnight train. We were travelling from Kyiv to Zaporizhzhia. I don't know much about it: metallurgy, chemistry, energy production, communist Soviet traditions, disappointment, depression – all those things that foreign experts talk about when they bring up the hopeless rift in Ukraine between the "pro-European West" and the "pro-Russian East." Zaporizhzhia is supposed to embody it, that "pro-Russian East" in its most obvious form.

To the contrary, the Euromaidan had been in existence there from the beginning. It was important for me to know this. In all those interviews I gave in Western media I repeated whenever I could: it's not true that people have risen only in Kyiv and in the west – but in Kharkiv, in Donetsk, and Zaporizhzhia too. And even in Simferopol. Yes, there are fewer of them there, but that shows their courage as even more commendable.

They were eagerly waiting for us in Zaporizhzhia. The hall in which we performed was extremely cold, unheated (this was a city of energy suppliers!), but it reacted with a special, acute anticipation and with an internal heat. So Mark was wrong to have been concerned about the health of his upright bass. After a moment of silence someone in the hall yelled "Glory to Ukraine!" and everyone responded.[3] "Glory to Zaporizhzhia!" I thought to myself.

That evening local anarchists gave me a book about Nestor Makhno[4] and his movement, signing it: "To Brother Yuri from the Zaporozhzhian Makhnovites." It made me want to believe even more about the common future of all the free people of our free country.

In reality, things were much worse. The nighttime city was swarming with armed gangs of semi-criminal thugs, the final fruits of the former regime. Someone was continuing to give them orders and money. Outside the window of our theatre hall a great dusk settled in with gunshots, police chases, home break-ins, and a very hazy perspective. Today, as I write these lines, it is even hazier.

And when we travelled to Odesa the following day, I once again became convinced of how neglected, robbed, abandoned, and still useless to anyone this boundless territory surrounding us was. It seemed to me that the top layer of the entire surface of the country needed to be scratched off, as mercilessly as possible, at least one and a half or two metres' worth, and that only after that, after having flattened out a newly formed and empty place, the thankless work of putting in true and proper foundations could begin.

The road got colder and darker.

9
Odesa

It had snowed in Odesa. The covered and somewhat stunned, colonial southern city nonetheless put up resistance with all of its bushes, trees, entryways, and balconies. The snow was temporary, but Odesa was, as always, immortal.

Two hours before our show we finished our final rehearsal and decided to go outside for a walk. The sea was somewhere close by. We made a right turn onto French Boulevard and ran down the steep stairs of some park straight onto the beach. Before it got completely dark outside, we wanted to see the snow falling onto the sea. It really did look black. We walked up to it closely, all the way to the tip of a breakwater.

Another step – and the future would have covered us, like a black wave.

March 2014

Notes

A Biographical Preface about the Author

1 I have borrowed some elements in this introduction from the introduction to my translation of the novel *Perverzion,* which appeared with North western University Press.

En Route Endeavours

1 "Erz-Herz-Perz," "The City-Ship," "Carpathologia Cosmophilica," "Time and Place, or My Last Territory," and "A Little Bit of Urban Studies" are from *Disorientation in Location.* "What Language Are You From: A Ukrainian Writer among the Temptations of Temporariness," "Meeting Place Germaschka," "Four Million for Our Agents," and "A Land of Dreams" are from *The Devil is Hiding in the Cheese.* "The Central-Eastern Revision" was published in *My Europe* (2000; with Andrzej Stasiuk). "The Star Absinthe: Notes on a Bitter Anniversary" was first published as "X, 1970–1986" in *Lexicon of Intimate Cities* (2011). "Love and Hatred in Kyiv" was published in January 2014 in *The New York Times* international edition. "Seven Hundred Fierce Days, or the Role of a Contrabass in the Revolution" was published in the 2014 German collection *Euromaidan: Was in der Ukraine auf dem Spiel steht.*

Author's Introduction

1 The only exception here is "Central Eastern Revision," which we agreed to place first because of its completely different scope and – one mustn't hide the truth – intimate confessional character (author's note).

The Central-Eastern Revision

1 This translation was originally published in a significantly abbreviated version in the journal *AGNI* under the title "Within Time, Down a River." The fuller revised version of the original essay first appeared in the book *Moia Evropa: dva esei pro naidyvnishu chastynu svitu* (Lviv: VNTL-Klasyka, 2005), which was coauthored with Polish writer Andrzej Stasiuk.

2 The Ukrainian word *klepsydra* also means a water clock. The author prefers the second meaning in the context of this essay of a roadside death notice, the kind placed on pillars and in public places in towns. Many thanks to Yuri for pointing this out to me.

3 Serbian writer Danilo Kis (1935–1989), best known for his prose works *A Tomb for Boris Davidovich* and *Encyclopedia of the Dead*. He died in 1989 of lung cancer.

4 The name for the northern and western part of the Austro-Hungarian Empire that included parts of Western Ukraine.

5 From "The Lay of the Love and Death of Cornet Christoph Rilke" (1899). The sentence in English translation is: My good mother, are you proud that I am carrying the flag?

6 In *The Foundations of a Yogi's Worldview*.

7 The Soviet Union with its fifteen republics comprised one-sixth of the world's landmass.

8 The Russian is an abbreviation meaning "Commander of the Division." Thanks to the author for pointing this out to me.

9 A term describing Germans who lived outside of the Reich.

10 An Austrian-German singer (1913–2004), who became popular in Nazi-era German films.

11 An acronym for Soviet counterintelligence groups formed by Stalin during World War II, colloquially standing for the phrase meaning "death to spies."

12 To each his own.

13 A Ukrainian folk instrument of the horn family.

14 Initials that stand for the Ukrainian National Republic, which lasted from 1917 until 1920.

15 A famous Ferris wheel in Vienna.

16 The actual village is in the Czech Republic and not in Austria.

17 The line from Horace's *Odes* (III.2.13), which means "it is sweet and proper to die for your fatherland."

18 The castle in Denmark made famous in Shakespeare's *Hamlet*.

19 Professional technical schools especially popular in Soviet times.

20 A Georgian white wine.

21 A reference to Bohdan Ihor Antonych's poem "Fialky" (Violets) in which the poet describes a telephone as a "snail made of ebony." Thanks to the author for revealing his source to me.

22 From the Third Prayer of St John Chrysostom before Holy Communion.

23 On the Monday after Easter it is a Ukrainian tradition (borrowed from pagan times) for eligible young men to sprinkle eligible young women with water as a purifying ritual.

24 From the Paschal troparion of the Byzantine Divine Liturgy.

Erz-Herz-Perz

1 A stereoscopic viewing device and precursor of film that originally went under the name Kaiserpanorama and was invented by August Furhmann. Some 250 of them were located throughout Europe. The one in Warsaw was called the Fotoplastikon.

2 The colours of the Ukrainian flag.

3 Myroslav Sichynsky (1887–1979), who was a terrorist in his youth and shot Polish Count Andrzej Potocki in 1908 in the latter's office. After managing to escape from a death sentence for the murder, he later emigrated to the United States, becoming president of the Ukrainian Workingman's Association (1933–1941). After later returning to Ukraine while it was still part of the USSR, he eventually returned to the US and died in an old age home in Michigan.

4 The online urban dictionary defines this as: "A coping mechanism used to survive an oppressive, chaotic, system of government which crushes the under classes to which the Švejker belongs." http://www.urbandictionary.com/define.php?term=%C5%A0vejk.

5 The Baroque Church of the Virgin Mary in Ivano-Frankivsk.

The City-Ship

1 The first three were Italian-born architects involved in many building projects in Lviv and its environs in the late sixteenth and early seventeenth century. Buonaccorsi was a defrocked Italian monk and humanist, who, under a papal death sentence for a plot on the life of the pope, took shelter in Lviv under the patronage of the local Polish bishop. He fell in love with a local barmaid in Lviv, writing her a series of love poems under the title *Fannientum*. He eventually became tutor to King Casimir IV in Poland and the first Polish ambassador to the Vatican (upon the accession of a new pope and the removal of the death sentence on him).

2 High Castle is a tall hill overlooking the city of Lviv that gives a panoramic view of the city. Remains of an old castle used for fortification lie at the top of it. Besides being a tourist attraction today, it is a spot for locals to visit with a bottle of champagne on special occasions like birthdays and weddings. For more information on it see: http://lvivecotour.com/the-high-castle-in-lviv/.

Carpathologia Cosmophilica

1 In West and South Slavic folklore, *planetnyki* are anthropomorphic but rarely seen evil spirits that live in rain and storm clouds and control the weather. They watch over life on earth and punish people for sins, sometimes abducting them. See the following source for a detailed description of them: http://bibliotekar.ru/mif/96.htm.
2 A village in the Carpathian Mountains in the Kosiv region of Ivano-Frankivsk oblast.
3 The *Tlumachnyi slovnyk ukrains'koi movy* defines "rakhman" (which comes from the Indian word Brahman) as: "An imaginary righteous Christian from a mythical land." http://eslovnik. com/%D1%80%D0%B0%D1%85%D0%BC%D0%B0%D0%BD.
4 For a discussion of the mythical Rahmans, see Valerii Voitovych, ed. *Antolohiia ukrains'koho mifu*, III (Ternopil: Vydavnytsvo "Bohdan," 2007), 193–4.
5 At that time the term "Ruthenian" (from the word Rus) was applied to Ukrainians since they were known as the descendants of the inhabitants of Kyivan Rus from the eighth–twelfth centuries. The term Ukrainian instead of Ruthenian became predominant in the nineteenth century.
6 Hutsuls are an ethnic group indigenous to the Carpathian Mountains known for their hearty independent lifestyle, brightly coloured manner of dress and lively dance music performed on folk instruments.
7 Prominent Ukrainian writer from Bukovyna in Western Ukraine (1834–1888). Most sources list his lengthy full name as: Osyp Dominik Hordynsky de Fedkovych.
8 The Gorals are highlanders, who live in Southern Poland. Lemkos are also a unique ethnic group with a colourful dialect who live in the Carpathians, mostly in present-day Poland and Slovakia.
9 A Russian pop star.

Time and Place, or My Final Territory

1 Written for the conference "Post-modern or post mortem?" (Lviv, January 1999).

2 Anatoly Onoprienko (1959–2013) was a mass murderer known as "The Beast of Ukraine," who confessed to killing fifty-two people. He was captured in 1996 and died in prison in 2013 of heart failure while serving a life sentence.

3 The image of "Kyiv tormented a hundredfold" comes from Ukrainian poet Pavlo Tychyna's poem "Both Bely and Blok, Esenin and Kliuev" (1919).

4 An admixture of Ukrainian and Russian spoken often among the working class.

A Little Bit of Urban Studies

1 The online Urban Dictionary defines this as: "A person from the former Soviet Union. In its derogatory form is used to denote those who have not completely liberated themselves from the totalitarian mindset." http://www.urbandictionary.com/define.php?term=sovok.

2 The Super Vuiky are a legendary rock band that performed in the Lviv underground during Soviet times. "Vuiky" is a slang term for Western Ukrainians with a patriotic fervour. Ihor Kalynets is a Ukrainian dissident poet from Lviv, who was imprisoned during Soviet times. And Hrytsko Chubai (1949–1982) was a legendary Ukrainian dissident poet and the father of Taras Chubai, the lead singer of the famous and now classic rock band Plach Yeremii (Jeremiah's Cry).

3 An experimental poet known for humour and linguistic play in his poetry.

4 The *Ievbaz* is the shortened form and the local name for the historical Jewish Bazaar (*Ievreis'kyi bazar*) in Kyiv, whose official name was Galician Bazaar, and was located next to the current Square of Victory (*ploshcha Peremohy*).

5 Lviv was founded in 1256 by Prince Danylo of Halych and named after his son Lev (Leo). It is known as the city of lions.

6 From Aphorism 146 in Nietszche's *Beyond Good and Evil*: "And when you gaze into the abyss, the abyss also gazes into you."

What Language Are You From: A Ukrainian Writer among the Temptations of Temporariness

1 This is known as the "Executed Renaissance" when over 700 Ukrainian writers and cultural activists were imprisoned and liquidated at Stalin's orders.

Meeting Place Germaschka

1 In the German alphabet, the letter β, known in English as a Sharp-S.

2 No foodstuff.

3 A typical Ukrainian first name and the name of the great Ukrainian national bard Taras Shevchenko.
4 Bimmer is slang for a BMW car.
5 German military intelligence from 1920–45.

A Land of Dreams

1 The hero Stanislav "Stakh" Perfetsky from Andrukhovych's novel *Perverzion*.
2 A 2002 novel by Polish writer Dorota Wasłowska. The title translates as *Polish-Russian War under a White-Red Flag*.

The Star Absinthe: Notes on a Bitter Anniversary

1 According to Our Guide, the roof of one of Prypiat's buildings had "Let the atom be a worker and not a soldier!" written on it in huge letters.
2 And why not "on a payment plan?"
3 The path to Prypiat goes through the former villages of Zalissia and Kopachi. The latter has, in fact, now been buried. In this manner a name crossed paths with its own destiny. [*Kopaty* means to dig in Ukrainian and a *kopach* is a person who digs.]
4 Levels of meaning *(Ger.)*
5 Valery Leontiev (b. 1949), Yuri Antonov (b. 1945), and Sofiia Rotaru (b. 1947) were among the most well-known pop singers in 1980s USSR. The latter's song *Lavanda* (Lavender) was a popular 1985 duet with Estonian singer Jaak Joala.

Love and Hatred in Kyiv

1 This appeared as an op-ed piece in the 29 January 2014 issue of the *New York Times* as "Love and Hatred in Kyiv." Ukrainians prefer the "Kyiv" spelling of the Ukrainian capital instead of the transliterated Russian version "Kiev."

Seven Hundred Fierce Days, or the Role of a Contrabass in the Revolution

1 Built in 1905 and originally named after the German poet and philosopher Friedrich Schiller (1759–1805), in 1954 it was renamed in honour of Ukrainian writer Olha Kobylianska (1863–1942).

2 Mezhyhiria is the name of a massive estate located on the banks of
the Dnipro River that was the residence of Ukrainian president Viktor
Yanukovych from 2002 until he fled the country in 2014 as a result of the
Euromaidan revolution. For many Ukrainians, the estate symbolized the
corruption of the Yanukovych regime and its insatiable thirst for riches
at the expense of the citizens it had sworn to serve. After Yanukovych's
escape, the estate became a popular museum of corruption open to the
public.

3 They responded with "Glory to the Heroes!"

4 Nestor Makhno (1888–1934) was an anarchist revolutionary who led an
army during the Russian Civil War. He has served as a symbol for some
anarchist and counter-cultural groups in post-Soviet Ukraine.

Index